Jesus' Journey to the Cross

A Love unto Death

Jesus' Journey to the Cross

A Love unto Death

Jeanne Kun

Published by The Word Among Us Press
7115 Guilford Road
Frederick, Maryland 21704
www.wau.org

www.wordamongus.org

17 16 15 14 13   4 5 6 7 8

ISBN: 978-1-59325-150-5

Nihil Obstat: The Rev. Michael Morgan, Chancellor
Censor Librorum
October 22, 2008
Imprimatur: +Most Rev. Victor Galeone, Bishop of St. Augustine
October 22, 2008

Scripture passages contained herein are from the New Revised Standard Version Bible: Catholic Edition, copyright © 1989, 1993, Division of Christian Education of the National Council of the Churches of Christ in the United States of America. Used by permission. All rights reserved. Excerpts from the English translation of the *Catechism of the Catholic Church* for use in the United States of America, copyright © 1994, United States Catholic Conference, Inc. —Libreria Editrice Vaticana. Used with permission.

Cover Design: David Crosson

Cover photograph: Anonymous, 20th century
Statue of the Crucifixion of Christ.
Location: Dingle Peninsula, County Kerry, Ireland
Photo Credit: Timothy McCarthy/Art Resource, NY

Made and printed in the United States of America.

Library of Congress Cataloging-in-Publication Data

Kun, Jeanne, 1951-
Jesus' journey to the cross : a love unto death / Jeanne Kun.
    p. cm.
ISBN 978-1-59325-150-5 (alk. paper)
1. Jesus Christ--Passion--Textbooks. I. Title.
BT431.3.K86 2009
232.96--dc22
                    2008040302

Contents

Welcome to
The Word Among Us
Keys to the Bible

Have you ever lost your keys? Everyone seems to have at least one "lost keys" story to tell. Maybe you had to break a window of your house or wait for the auto club to let you into your car. Whatever you had to do probably cost you—in time, energy, money, or all three. Keys are definitely important items to have on hand!

The guides in The Word Among Us Keys to the Bible series are meant to provide you with a handy set of keys that can "unlock" the treasures of the Scriptures for you. Scripture is God's living word. Within its pages we meet the Lord. So as we study and meditate on Scripture and unlock its many treasures, we discover the riches it contains—and in the process, we grow in intimacy with God.

Since 1982 *The Word Among Us* magazine has helped Catholics develop a deeper relationship with the Lord through daily meditations that bring the Scriptures to life. More than ever, Catholics today desire to read and pray with the Scriptures, and many have begun to form small faith-sharing groups to explore the Bible together.

We designed the Keys to the Bible series after conducting a survey among our magazine readers to learn what they wanted in a Catholic Bible study. We found that they were looking for easy-to-understand, faith-filled materials that approach Scripture from a clearly Catholic perspective. Moreover, they wanted a Bible study that shows them how they can apply what they learn from Scripture to their everyday lives. They also asked for sessions that they can complete in an hour or two.

Our goal was to design a simple, easy-to-use Bible study guide that is also challenging and thought provoking. We hope that this guide fulfills those admittedly ambitious goals. We are confident, however, that taking the time to go through this guide—whether by yourself, with a friend, or in a small group—will be a worthwhile endeavor that will bear fruit in your life.

How to Use the Guides in This Series

The study guides in the Keys to the Bible series are divided into six sessions that each deal with a particular aspect of the topic. Before starting the first session, take the time to read the introduction, which sets the stage for the sessions that follow.

Whether you use this guide for personal reflection and study, as part of a faith-sharing group, or as an aid in your prayer time, be sure to begin each session with prayer. Ask God to open his word to you and to speak to you personally. Read each Scripture passage slowly and carefully. Then, take as much time as you need to meditate on the passage and pursue any thoughts it brings to mind. When you are ready, move on to the accompanying commentary, which offers various insights into the text.

Two sets of questions are included in each session to help you "mine" the Scripture passage and discover its relevance to your life. Those under the heading "Understand!" focus on the text itself and help you grasp what it means. Occasionally a question allows for a variety of answers and is meant to help you explore the passage from several angles. "Grow!" questions are intended to elicit a personal response by helping you examine your life in light of the values and truths that you uncover through your study of the Scripture passage and its setting. Under the headings "Reflect!" and "Act!" we offer suggestions to help you respond concretely to the challenges posed by the passage.

Finally, pertinent quotations from the Fathers of the Church as well as insights from contemporary writers appear throughout each session. Coupled with relevant selections from the *Catechism of the Catholic Church* and information about the history, geography, and culture of first-century Palestine, these selections (called

"In the Spotlight") add new layers of understanding and insight to your study.

As is true with any learning resource, you will benefit the most from this study by writing your answers to the questions in the spaces provided. The simple act of writing can help you formulate your thoughts more clearly—and will also give you a record of your reflections and spiritual growth that you can return to in the future to see how much God has accomplished in your life. End your reading or study with a prayer thanking God for what you have learned—and ask the Holy Spirit to guide you in living out the call you have been given as a Christian in the world today.

Although the Scripture passages to be studied and the related verses for your reflection are printed in full in each guide (from the New Revised Standard Version: Catholic Edition), you will find it helpful to have a Bible on hand for looking up other passages and cross-references or for comparing different translations.

The format of the guides in The Word Among Us Keys to the Bible series is especially well suited for use in small groups. Some recommendations and practical tips for using this guide in a Bible discussion group are offered on pages 108–111.

We hope that this guide will unlock the meaning of the Scriptures for you. As you accompany Jesus on his journey to the cross, may the Holy Spirit draw you closer to the heavenly Father, increase your love for him, and deepen your understanding of Jesus' redeeming work in your life.

The Word Among Us Press

Introduction
Divine Love Revealed

In *Jesus' Journey to the Cross: A Love unto Death,* you will follow Jesus from his entrance into Jerusalem, through his last meal with his apostles, his struggle in Gethsemane, his arrest and trial, to his crucifixion and, finally, his resurrection from the dead. This thoughtful look at the person and character of Jesus is meant to stir your heart to awesome wonder and gratitude. As you read and study the gospel descriptions of the final days and hours of Jesus' life, you will see his divine love revealed in his total surrender and self-emptying and in his victorious resurrection. It's in contemplating Jesus' journey to the cross and beyond, to that the empty tomb, that we can experience his intimate personal love for us. And we become certain that we are loved with the eternal love of God, a love that will never fade or pass away.

Jesus' journey to the cross was actually set in motion long before the events of those final days in Jerusalem. It began in the garden of Eden, when sin and suffering, sickness and death came into the world through Adam and Eve's disobedience. In that moment, humankind's communion with God was broken, and the world became alienated from its Creator, infected by evil and entrapped in Satan's deceits and allurements. Yet, full of love and mercy, God reversed the consequences of Adam and Eve's fall by sending his own divine Son into the world to conquer sin, Satan, and death, and restore the human race to union with himself. "God so loved the world that he gave his only Son, . . . in order that the world might be saved through him" (John 3:16-17).

No Greater Love Than This

Jesus, the eternal Son of God, assented to his Father's plan for our salvation and willingly took on human flesh to fulfill that plan. In fact, "the desire to embrace his Father's plan of redeeming love inspired Jesus' whole life, for his redemptive passion was the very reason for his Incarnation" (*Catechism of the Catholic Church*, 607).

In the incarnation, Jesus took on a human nature like ours so that, by his crucifixion and resurrection, he could rescue us from eternal death. Because of Jesus' great love and his total submission to the Father, even to death, the human race was redeemed. Our relationship to the Father has been restored, and we are able to share again in eternal life. As the *Catechism* notes,

> By embracing in his human heart the Father's love for men, Jesus "loved them to the end," for "greater love has no man than this, that a man lay down his life for his friends" [John 13:1; 15:13]. In suffering and death his humanity became the free and perfect instrument of his divine love which desires the salvation of men. Indeed, out of love for his Father and for men, whom the Father wants to save, Jesus freely accepted his Passion and death: "No one takes [my life] from me, but I lay it down of my own accord" [John 10:18]. (609)

Accompanying Jesus

Years of ordinary life and faithful obedience to his earthly parents lay between Jesus' birth in the stable at Bethlehem and his last journey to Jerusalem. It was in these years that Jesus matured in his human character to face the task his heavenly Father asked him to carry out (see Luke 2:51–52).

When we recall Jesus' earthly life and, most especially, his journey to the cross, whether in prayerful meditation, in Bible study, or in the celebration of the Eucharist, we are not just recalling the historical account of an obscure Jewish carpenter, nor are we simply reminding ourselves of the significance of this man's death and resurrection. Far more than a memorial service or a theological review, our reflection on Jesus' passion and death is an opportunity to *accompany* Jesus on his path.

When we read and study the gospel accounts of Jesus' final days or hear them read at Mass as we celebrate the Eucharist, we should try to *live* these events with Jesus as if they are happening now, in the present. For it's as we reflect on the scenes of Jesus' passion that we live out anew with him the mystery of the redemption he won for us. And reliving the mystery of redemption means experiencing its transforming power in our own lives, for through the cross we have been set free from bondage to sin—released from Satan's stranglehold by the death and resurrection of our Lord Jesus Christ.

Reflection on the passion of Jesus should be a regular part of our spiritual life. Indeed, many of the greatest saints—among them Thomas Aquinas, Teresa of Ávila, Clare of Assisi, and Paul of the Cross—found inspiration and strength by meditating on the gospels' descriptions of Jesus' life and death, and they encouraged others to do the same.

But it is especially during the season of Lent that the Church urges us to contemplate Christ's passion and death and its meaning for our lives. Through our Lenten prayer and practices, we become more open to the Lord's work in us as he purifies our hearts and helps us to love others with his love, free of sin and selfishness. And as we grasp the full truth and reality of our redemption, our desire will grow stronger to be obedient to God's will in all things, just as Jesus was perfectly obedient in submitting to the Father's plan for our salvation.

The Scriptures Fulfilled

In the study sessions included in this guide, we will read not only many of the New Testament's gospel accounts concerning Jesus' passion but also several Old Testament prophecies that pointed to it. The prophetic words of Zechariah find their fulfillment in Jesus' entry into Jerusalem, and in the "suffering servant of God" foretold by Isaiah we recognize the One crucified for our sake.

Moreover, many realities and events recorded in the Old Testament are "types" or prefigurements of Christ and his redeeming acts. In an imperfect and transitory way, images and incidents in the history of the ancient Israelites prefigured perfect and eternal realities that are fully revealed or made complete in Christ. As the *Catechism* explains, "'figures' (types) . . . announce [Christ] in the deeds, words, and symbols of the first covenant. By this re-reading in the Spirit of Truth, starting from Christ, the figures are unveiled" (1094). For example, the manna that God gave the Israelites in the desert foreshadows the Eucharist that Jesus instituted at the Last Supper. The Passover lamb of the Exodus foreshadows Jesus, the Lamb of God who takes away the sins of the world.

Growing in an understanding and appreciation of how Old Testament prophecies, types, and events point toward fulfillment in the New Testament will broaden our understanding and appreciation of God and the marvelous plan of salvation his Son has carried out for us.

Our Own Journey as Followers of Jesus

So great was Jesus' love for the Father and for us that nothing could turn him aside from meeting his death on Golgotha. We have been called to follow in Jesus' footsteps—and that call to be his disciples reaches into every aspect of our daily lives: "Those who love their life lose it, and those who hate their life in this world will keep it for eternal life. Whoever serves me must follow me, and where I am, there will my servant be also" (John 12:25-26).

Jesus asks us to follow him with this same resolve and abandonment to the will of God made possible by faith in his fatherly care. Discipleship entails a costly emptying of self, but its rewards are great, for we enjoy the companionship of the One who loves us beyond all measure.

Jesus did not try to take an easier road or avoid the journey to the cross. He "set his face" to Jerusalem (see Luke 9:51) and to his suffering, not turning aside from it. Today he still challenges each of us to this same perseverance, but he does not expect us to make this journey on our own: he has gone this way before us and is there to accompany us each step of our way. And because of the resurrection, we know that our journey will end on that final day, when we will gaze with unveiled faces on the glory of the Lord (see 2 Corinthians 3:18).

Jeanne Kun

"Your King Is Coming to You"

Matthew 20:17-19; 21:1-11

^{20:17} While Jesus was going up to Jerusalem, he took the twelve disciples aside by themselves, and said to them on the way, ¹⁸"See, we are going up to Jerusalem, and the Son of Man will be handed over to the chief priests and scribes, and they will condemn him to death; ¹⁹then they will hand him over to the Gentiles to be mocked and flogged and crucified; and on the third day he will be raised.". . .

> The Kingdom was indeed coming; he who was to come—the Messiah—was coming. At last. But the donkey should have warned them that it would not be the kingdom of their dreams—he was coming peaceably, not as for war.
> —**Frank Sheed,** *To Know Christ Jesus*

^{21:1}When they had come near Jerusalem and had reached Bethphage, at the Mount of Olives, Jesus sent two disciples, ²saying to them, "Go into the village ahead of you, and immediately you will find a donkey tied, and a colt with her; untie them and bring them to me. ³If anyone says anything to you, just say this, 'The Lord needs them.' And he will send them immediately." ⁴This took place to fulfill what had been spoken through the prophet, saying,

⁵ "Tell the daughter of Zion,
      Look, your king is coming to you,
         humble, and mounted on a donkey,
            and on a colt, the foal of a donkey."

⁶The disciples went and did as Jesus had directed them; ⁷they brought the donkey and the colt, and put their cloaks on them, and he sat on them. ⁸A very large crowd spread their cloaks on the road, and others cut branches from the trees and spread them on the road. ⁹The crowds that went ahead of him and that followed were shouting,

   "Hosanna to the Son of David!
   Blessed is the one who comes in the name of the Lord!

Hosanna in the highest heaven!"

[10]When he entered Jerusalem, the whole city was in turmoil, asking, "Who is this?" [11]The crowds were saying, "This is the prophet Jesus from Nazareth in Galilee."

(See also Mark 11:1-11; Luke 19:29-40; John 12:12-19.)

When the days drew near for him to be taken up, [Jesus] set his face to go to Jerusalem" (Luke 9:51). Centuries earlier the obedience of Yahweh's "servant" had been foretold in similar words: "I have set my face like flint / and I know that I shall not be put to shame; / he who vindicates me is near" (Isaiah 50:7-8). Jesus had gone up to Jerusalem before—perhaps even yearly to celebrate the Passover in accord with the law (see Luke 2:41)—but this journey would be his last. Now, resolutely headed toward the Holy City, Jesus approached his own Passover, the culmination of his mission finally at hand. Once again he told his apostles, as he had earlier, of his impending death and resurrection. And yet again, they failed to understand him (see Matthew 20:17-19; Mark 10:32-34; Luke 18:31-34).

Jesus sent two of his disciples ahead into the village of Bethphage to fetch a donkey and its colt for him, instructing them, "If anyone says anything to you, just say this, 'The Lord needs them'" (Matthew 21:3). Archbishop Fulton Sheen once commented on the irony of such a statement coming from the Son of God:

> Perhaps no greater paradox was ever written than this—on the one hand the sovereignty of the Lord, and on the other His "need." This combination of Divinity and dependence, of possession and poverty was the consequence of the Word becoming flesh. Truly, He who was rich became poor for our sakes, that we might be rich. He borrowed a boat from a fisherman from which to preach; He borrowed barley loaves and fishes from a boy to feed the multitude; . . . and now He borrowed an ass on which to enter Jerusalem. Sometimes God preempts and requisitions the things of man, as if to remind him that everything is a gift from Him. It is sufficient for those who know Him to hear: "The Lord hath need of it." (*Life of Christ*)

It was popularly believed by many Jews that the Messiah would come at Passover time to establish his kingdom. In Galilee, Jesus had avoided a crowd's attempt to crown him king (see John 6:15), and he refused to be called Messiah. But now, by riding into David's city on a donkey rather than walking as pilgrims usually did, he openly proclaimed his identity as the long-awaited one. With this symbolic action he fulfilled the ancient prophecies about the coming of Israel's Messiah-King: "Lo, your king comes to you; / triumphant and victorious is he, / humble and riding on a donkey, / on a colt, the foal of a donkey" (Zechariah 9:9; see also Isaiah 62:11; John 12:15).

Jubilant crowds greeted Jesus with loud cries of "Hosanna!" They spread their cloaks and palm branches on the ground in his path as they hailed him as "Son of David" (Matthew 21:9) and celebrated his kingship. In doing so, they were recalling the promises Yahweh had made to King David, promises of an eternal dynasty and of a kingdom that would last forever. Despite the disasters and sins of the monarchy that unfolded after the reign of David, the Jewish people had for centuries kept alive the hope that these promises would be fulfilled by a future "hero-king." Descended from David, this anointed leader or "Messiah" would free Israel from the yoke of foreign oppression, restore the kingdom, establish perfect justice, and revive the glorious reign of David forever.

> Ultimately, God's promise to David would be fulfilled through the death and resurrection of Jesus Christ.

Burning with nationalism, many in the crowd that first Palm Sunday looked to "the prophet Jesus from Nazareth" (Matthew 21:11) as a political savior. But Jesus did not come on a warhorse to liberate the land from Roman occupation and establish an independent Jewish state. Rather, he came astride a young ass, on a mission of peace—and he would come into his kingly reign through the cross.

Jesus wept over the fact that Jerusalem had failed to recognize the time of its visitation (see Luke 19:41-44). Although at the moment the crowds wildly greeted him, the people of Israel misunderstood the true meaning of Jesus' messiahship. Yet their faith would be vindicated: ultimately, God's promise to David would be fulfilled through the death and resurrection of Jesus Christ.

Understand!

1. Note several ways in which Jesus' entrance into Jerusalem points to his messianic identity and role. Why, in your opinion, was it important for Jesus to demonstrate that Old Testament prophecies regarding the Messiah were fulfilled in him?

_____

_____

_____

_____

_____

_____

2. What paradox is reflected in Zechariah's descriptive prophecy? What meaning or significance do you see in the donkey beyond its prophetic undertones?

_____

_____

_____

_____

_____

_____

3. How would you describe the atmosphere and mood of the crowd as Jesus entered Jerusalem? How do you think this affected Jesus?

_____

_____

_____

_____

_____

_____

_____

4. Read 2 Samuel 7:12-16; Psalm 89:3-4; and Matthew 22:41-45. In light of these texts, why do you think Jesus' entrance into Jerusalem provoked such an intense reaction among the people? Why did they hail him as the "Son of David (Matthew 21:9)?

_____

_____

_____

_____

_____

_____

5. Read Luke 19:29-40 to gain another perspective on Jesus' entry into Jerusalem. What information does Luke supply that is not noted by Matthew? What does the exchange between the Pharisees and Jesus in Luke 19:39-40 add to your understanding of Jesus and his character?

_____

_____

_____

_____

_____

_____

▶ In the Spotlight
In the Words of the Saints

> Let us run to accompany Christ as he hastens toward his passion, and imitate those who met him then, not by covering his path with garments, olive branches or palms, but by doing all we can to prostrate ourselves before him by being humble and by trying to live as he would wish. Then we shall be able to receive the Word at his coming, and God, whom no limits can contain, will be within us.
> —St. Andrew of Crete

> Jesus . . . makes do with a poor animal for a throne. I don't know about you; but I am not humiliated to acknowledge that in the Lord's eyes I am a beast of burden: "I am like a donkey in your presence; but I am continually with you. You hold my right hand" (Psalm 73:22-23), you take me by the bridle.
> —St. Josemaría Escrivá

> With his entry into Jerusalem, Christ begins his journey of love and sorrow, which is the Cross. Look to him with renewed and zealous faith. Follow him! He does not promise illusory happiness; on the contrary, in order for you to achieve authentic human and spiritual maturity, he invites you to follow his demanding example, making his exacting choices your own.
> —Pope John Paul II

Grow!

1. Jesus came resolutely to Jerusalem, knowing that he would be crucified there. Recall a time when you "set your face like flint" (Isaiah 50:7) and persevered in doing something that you felt the Lord was asking of you, even though you knew you might be met with

criticism or a negative response. How did you experience God at work in this incident? What fruit came from your obedience?

_____

_____

_____

_____

_____

_____

2. What skills, talents, or resources has the Lord asked you to put at his disposal because he has "need" of them? In what areas might you be more generous and allow him to use you more effectively?

_____

_____

_____

_____

_____

_____

3. Imagine yourself in Jerusalem on that first Palm Sunday. What role would you have played? If Jesus were to enter your town today, how do you think various people—for example, politicians, CEOs, churchgoers, the homeless, children, scholars—would respond to him?

_____

_____

_____

_____

_____

_____

4. Are you comfortable or do you feel inhibited in expressing your love for Jesus in front of family members and friends? Strangers? How do you feel when others publicly show their devotion to the Lord? Inspired? Embarrassed? Explain.

_____

_____

_____

_____

_____

_____

_____

5. Think of a situation, relationship, or area of your life that is difficult for you to surrender to the Lord. Write a prayer to praise and thank Jesus for the ways that you experience his kingship, and to ask him for grace to submit this difficulty fully to his rule and authority over you.

_____

_____

_____

_____

_____

_____

_____

▶ In the Spotlight
Contemporary Voices

The gospel texts speak of [Jesus'] entrance into Jerusalem in terms that are redolent of a *parousia*—the arrival of an emperor in a triumphant victory parade with songs of celebration and welcome. In thus commemorating [in the Palm Sunday liturgy] this past event in the life of Jesus, we are at the same time expressing our faith that "he will come again in glory to judge the living and the dead." It is then that the entire world will understand the meaning of what transpired that day in Jerusalem. Jesus, in an anticipatory symbolic act, declared his Messiahship by entering Jerusalem. He came to fulfill all that the Father willed his Messiah to accomplish on the way to becoming king. This faith vision is meant to illumine our understanding of Jesus' journey, through the abasement and pain of the cross, to his present state at God's right hand.

—Francis Martin, *The Fire in the Cloud: Lenten Meditations*

Reflect!

1. Upon entering a city, monarchs are often welcomed by an honor guard or parade. Streets and buildings may be decorated with banners for the royal visit, and crowds greet the royal person's arrival with enthusiastic shouts of acclamation. Respect is also shown to monarchs by gestures and honorific titles. For example, men bow and women curtsey ("make a courtesy") when presented to a queen, and a king is usually addressed as "Your Majesty."

   How have you welcomed Jesus into your life as your king and Lord? How do you show him honor and reverence? Consider the postures used and the titles given to God in liturgical worship.

2. Reflect on the following Scripture passages to deepen your understanding of how God is given honor and acclaim in worship:

   David blessed the LORD in the presence of all the assembly; David said: "Blessed are you, O LORD, the God of our ancestor Israel, forever and ever. Yours, O LORD, are the greatness, the power, the glory, the victory, and the majesty; for all that is in the heavens and on the earth is yours; yours is the kingdom, O LORD, and you are exalted as head above all. Riches and honor come from you, and you rule over all. In your hand are power and might; and it is in your hand to make great and to give strength to all. And now, our God, we give thanks to you and praise your glorious name.

—1 Chronicles 29:10-13

Solomon assembled the elders of Israel and all the heads of the tribes, the leaders of the ancestral houses of the people of Israel, in Jerusalem, to bring up the ark of the covenant of the LORD out of the city of David, which is Zion. . . . Then the priests brought the ark of the covenant of the LORD to its place, in the inner sanctuary of the house, in the most holy place, underneath the wings of the cherubim. . . . It was the duty of the trumpeters and singers to make themselves heard in unison in praise and thanksgiving to the LORD, and when the song was raised, with trumpets and cymbals and other musical instruments, in praise to the LORD,

"For he is good,
for his steadfast love endures forever,"
the house, the house of the LORD, was filled with a cloud, so that the priests could not stand to minister because of the cloud; for the glory of the LORD filled the house of God.

—2 Chronicles 5:2, 7, 13-14

O give thanks to the LORD, call on his name,
make known his deeds among the peoples.
Sing to him, sing praises to him;
tell of all his wonderful works.
Glory in his holy name;
let the hearts of those who seek the LORD rejoice.

—Psalm 105:1-3

I [John] looked, and there was a great multitude that no one could count, from every nation, from all tribes and peoples and languages, standing before the throne and before the Lamb, robed in white, with palm branches in their hands. They cried out in a loud voice, saying,

"Salvation belongs to our God who is seated on the throne, and to the Lamb!"

And all the angels stood around the throne and around the elders and the four living creatures, and they fell on their faces before the throne and worshiped God, singing,

"Amen! Blessing and glory and wisdom
and thanksgiving and honor
and power and might
be to our God forever and ever! Amen."

—Revelation 7:9-12

▶ In the Spotlight
Hosanna!

"Hosanna" is the Greek and English transliteration of the Hebrew entreaty *hosa na*, meaning "Save (us)," "Give salvation," or "Help (us)!" Originally the word simply expressed a plea for deliverance or a cry for rescue from danger (see 2 Samuel 14:4), but over time it became an invocation of blessing and even an acclamation of praise:

Save us, we beseech you, O LORD!
    O LORD, we beseech you, give us success!
Blessed is the one who comes in the name of the LORD.
    We bless you from the house of the LORD.
(Psalm 118:25-26)

Many biblical scholars surmise that Psalm 118 depicts a celebration of a king's victory in the Temple. Verse 27 exhorts: "Bind the festal procession with branches." Recalling that psalm, the crowds who welcomed Jesus with hosannas and waved palm branches before him may have expected that he would proceed to the Temple and affirm his kingship at the altar by declaring, as in verse 19, "Open to me the gates of righteousness."

In the Eucharistic liturgy we recite or sing the *Sanctus*, "Hosanna in the highest! Blessed is he who comes in the name of the Lord." Each time we do so, we celebrate and proclaim anew Christ's kingship.

Act!

Gestures speak loudly and often express our feelings better than words. The crowds jubilantly spread their cloaks and palm branches on the road before Jesus as he entered Jerusalem. David leapt and danced with joyful abandon before the ark of the Lord (see 2 Samuel 6:14, 16). The wise men knelt and prostrated themselves in homage before the infant Jesus (see Matthew 2:11). Mary of Bethany poured precious ointment over Jesus' feet and wiped them with her hair (see John 12:3).

This week add some "body language" to your prayer times to express your worship and love of God. Lift your arms in praise, bow in reverence, dance with joy, lie prostrate on the floor, or even march around as a symbolic way of sharing in Jesus' victory over sin and death. Don't be constrained by conventions and more familiar forms of prayer. You may want to do this when you're alone so you don't feel inhibited by the presence of others. Spontaneous and heartfelt gestures can lead you into a deeper relationship with the Lord.

From the *Catechism of the Catholic Church*

How will Jerusalem welcome her Messiah? Although Jesus had always refused popular attempts to make him king, he chooses the time and prepares the details for his messianic entry into the city of "his father David." Acclaimed as son of David, as the one who brings salvation . . . , the "King of glory" enters his City "riding on an ass." Jesus conquers the Daughter of Zion, a figure of his Church, neither by ruse nor by violence, but by the humility that bears witness to the truth. And so the subjects of his kingdom on that day are children and God's poor, who acclaim him as had the angels when they announced him to the shepherds. (559)

Jesus went up to Jerusalem voluntarily, knowing well that there he would die a violent death because of the opposition of sinners (cf. Hebrews 12:3). (569)

Jesus' entry into Jerusalem manifests the coming of the kingdom that the Messiah-King, welcomed into his city by children and the humble of heart, is going to accomplish by the Passover of his Death and Resurrection. (570)

A Banquet
of Love

Matthew 26:17-19, 26-30

celebrated during Passover
1 week

¹⁷ On the first day of Unleavened Bread the disciples came to Jesus, saying, "Where do you want us to make the preparations for you to eat the Passover?" ¹⁸He said, "Go into the city to a certain man, and say to him, 'The Teacher says, My time is near; I will keep the Passover at your house with my disciples.'" ¹⁹So the disciples did as Jesus had directed them, and they prepared the Passover meal. . . .

> I hunger for the bread of God, the flesh of Jesus Christ. . . . I long to drink of his blood, the gift of unending love.
>
> —St. Ignatius of Antioch

²⁶ While they were eating, Jesus took a loaf of bread, and after blessing it he broke it, gave it to the disciples, and said, "Take, eat; this is my body." ²⁷Then he took a cup, and after giving thanks he gave it to them, saying, "Drink from it, all of you; ²⁸for this is my blood of the covenant, which is poured out for many for the forgiveness of sins. ²⁹I tell you, I will never again drink of this fruit of the vine until that day when I drink it new with you in my Father's kingdom."

³⁰ When they had sung the hymn, they went out to the Mount of Olives.

(See also Mark 14:12-17, 22-26 and Luke 22:7-20.)

1 Corinthians 11:23-26

²³ I [Paul] received from the Lord what I also handed on to you, that the Lord Jesus on the night when he was betrayed took a loaf of bread, ²⁴and when he had given thanks, he broke it and said, "This is my body that is for you. Do this in remembrance of me." ²⁵In the same way he took the cup also, after supper, saying, "This cup is the new covenant in my blood. Do this, as often as you drink it, in remembrance of me." ²⁶For as often as you eat this bread and drink the cup, you proclaim the Lord's death until he comes.

J ust as Jesus had made careful preparations to obtain a donkey for his prophetic entry into Jerusalem, so too did he make very precise arrangements to celebrate the Passover with his apostles (see Matthew 26:17-19; Luke 22:7-13).* The culmination of Jesus' mission was near: the Passover festival was the time when he would "be handed over to be crucified" (Matthew 26:2). As the Evangelist John tells us, "Jesus knew that his hour had come to depart from this world and go to the Father. Having loved his own who were in the world, he loved them to the end" (13:1). The shadow of the cross had already darkened the upper room and fell across the supper table as Jesus spoke of his betrayal (see Matthew 26:21-25) and of his departure (see John 16:16-20). Aware that this evening was the eve of his passion, in his final hours Jesus manifested his love in an extraordinary way, giving us his body and blood—an everlasting memorial to the ultimate sacrifice, his death on the cross.

The first Passover was the night of the ancient Israelites' deliverance from their bondage in Egypt, and each year devout Jews commemorate God's saving deed with the festive Passover meal, just as God had commanded Moses to do (see Exodus 12:1-8, 11-14). As the *Catechism of the Catholic Church* explains,

> By celebrating the Last Supper with his apostles in the course of the Passover meal, Jesus gave the Jewish Passover its definitive meaning. Jesus' passing over to his father by his death and Resurrection, the new Passover, is anticipated in the Supper and celebrated in the Eucharist, which fulfills the Jewish Passover and anticipates the final Passover of the Church in the glory of the kingdom. (1340)

After Jesus and his closest friends had gathered to share this special meal together, he gave them bread and wine, transformed into his body and blood. This sacrificial action anticipated the events of the next day, when his body would be nailed to the cross on Calvary and his blood would be shed there. As Jesus offered the cup to his apostles, he told them, "This is my blood of the covenant, which is poured out for many for the forgiveness of sins" (Matthew 26:28). In Egypt, the blood of a lamb put on their doorposts had protected the Israelites (see Exodus 12:7, 13). At Sinai, Moses had sprinkled the blood of an animal sacrifice on the Israelites to consecrate them as God's holy people and to ratify God's covenant with them (see 24:4-8). Now Jesus offered his own lifeblood in the sacrifice of the Eucharist and of Calvary as the atonement for our sins. In doing so, he sealed a new covenant, the covenant of our redemption.

Our union with Jesus—"communion" with him—is made actual in the Eucharist but will only be made complete in heaven. The bread and wine that Jesus gave his disciples as his body and blood are a foretaste of the wedding feast of the Lamb in the heavenly Jerusalem (see Revelation 19:9). Jesus' words, "I will never again drink of this fruit of the vine until that day when I drink it new with you in my Father's

> "Communion" with Jesus is made actual in the Eucharist but will only be made complete in heaven.

kingdom" (Matthew 26:29), not only point to his impending death but also look beyond it to future glory, to the age to come when he will drink from the cup with us at the heavenly banquet table.

St. Paul's description of the institution of the Eucharist is the earliest one that we have. It was recorded around the year 57, before the gospels were written, little more than twenty-five years after Jesus' death. In his first letter to the Corinthians, Paul "handed on" to them the teaching of the apostles. What he "received from the Lord" (11:23) is a technical expression meaning what Paul had received through the apostolic Tradition, which goes back to the Lord himself. And it is Paul's great proclamation of the mystery of faith that we echo at the celebration of Mass: "For as often as you eat this bread and drink the cup, you proclaim the Lord's death until he comes" (see 11:26).

*Scholars point to the different calendars and variant ways of calculating dates that were used by the Sadducees, Pharisees, and other Jewish groups of Jesus' day as the most likely reason for the discrepancy between the synoptic gospels and the Gospel of St. John. The synoptic gospels describe the Last Supper as a Passover meal, and John places the meal on the evening before Passover, with Jesus' crucifixion occurring during the day of Preparation for the coming Passover, which would be celebrated after sunset (see John 19:13-14).

Understand!

1. Read Luke's description (22:7-13) of the arrangements Jesus made to celebrate the Passover meal. What details are included by Luke that are not present in Matthew's account? Why do you think Jesus took such concern for where and how this meal with his closest friends would take place?

_____

_____

_____

_____

_____

_____

_____

2. What similarities do you see between the events of the first Passover (read Exodus, chapter 12) and Jesus' actions at the Last Supper? What new significance did Jesus give to the Passover meal when he departed from the rituals and blessings used by Jews when they celebrated it?

_____

_____

_____

_____

_____

_____

_____

3. Why did Jesus have to offer his blood "for the forgiveness of sins" (Matthew 26:28) at the Last Supper and on Calvary? Explain what it means to you personally that you have been "ransomed from the futile ways inherited from your ancestors, not with perishable things like silver or gold, but with the precious blood of Christ, like that of a lamb without defect or blemish" (1 Peter 1:18-19).

_____

_____

_____

_____

_____

_____

_____

4. Why, in your opinion, did Jesus tell his apostles, "Do this in remembrance of me" (1 Corinthians 11:24-25; Luke 22:19)? How is the Eucharist a memorial meal? A sacrificial meal? An *agape* meal, that is, a "love" meal?

_____

_____

_____

_____

_____

_____

_____

5. What does it mean to proclaim Jesus' death until he comes (see 1 Corinthians 11:26)? How do we do this through our actions? How do these words of St. Paul point to the future and instill hope in you?

_____

_____

_____

_____

_____

_____

_____

▶ In the Spotlight
Wisdom from the Church Fathers

As the bread, which comes from the earth, on receiving the invocation of God, is no longer common bread but Eucharist, and is then both earthly and heavenly; so our bodies, after partaking of the Eucharist, are no longer corruptible, having the hope of the eternal resurrection.
—St. Irenaeus

Many mothers there are who after the pains of childbirth give their children to strangers to nurse. But Christ could not endure that his children should be fed by others. He nourishes us himself with his own blood and in all ways makes us one with himself.
—St. John Chrysostom

When, therefore, we eat the holy flesh of Christ, the Savior of us all, and drink his precious blood, we have life in us, being made as it were, one with him, and abiding in him, and possessing him also in us.
—St. Cyril of Alexandria

Grow!

1. In the Eucharist we are united to the same One who delivered Israel from slavery and oppression in Egypt. From what "slavery" to sin or oppression has Jesus freed you? What else—perhaps a sin pattern, attitude, or habit—could you ask Jesus to deliver you from?

_____

_____

_____

_____

_____

_____

2. In the Eucharist Jesus shows his tremendous love for us. We respond by sharing our love with his body, our brothers and sisters in Christ. How do you share your love for Jesus and the Eucharist with others? What changes could you make in your life to increase your opportunities to share Jesus' love?

_____

_____

_____

_____

_____

_____

3. The Greek word *eucharistein* means "thanksgiving." How is your participation at Mass and your reception of Communion a

conscious act of giving thanks to God? What else could you do to
show your gratitude to the Lord for all he has done for you?

_____

_____

_____

_____

_____

_____

_____

4. What does St. Paul's description of the institution of the Eucharist
in 1 Corinthians 11:23-26 suggest to you about the importance
of the witness and teaching of the apostles? About the role of the
Church in preserving the apostolic Tradition?

_____

_____

_____

_____

_____

_____

5. When you receive Christ's body and blood in the Eucharist, how
aware are you of the grace and strength that come from sharing
in his divine life? When has the Eucharist strengthened you during a particular difficult time? What steps can you take to increase
your faith in the power of this sacrament?

_____

_____

_____

_____

_____

_____

▶ In the Spotlight
The Most Sacred of Meals

Father John J. Gayton, from the Diocese of Wilmington, Delaware, is a military chaplain who serves U.S. troops in Iraq.

I am traveling with a military convoy, making pastoral visits to the 2nd Battalion, 7th Marine Regiment. First stop is their Forward Operating Base in a central Iraq town.

There is no separate space to set apart for Mass or a religious service, so I set up in the area where the Marines eat and recreate, which is also used as the triage area for the wounded. Foot patrols are returning after an eight-hour shift through the night, and others were departing on their shift. Marines and Corpsmen are rushing about trying to get a bite to eat and get ready to sleep for a few hours. Despite the intense operational tempo and grueling schedule, a group of Marines led by their company commanding officer gather in the corner for the Mass.

From a kit smaller than a shoebox that I carry on my back, I pull out the olive green altar linens and the compact parts of a brushed steel crucifix, chalice, and paten. The altar is a wooden bench—the best piece of furniture in the room. There is no singing, no stained glass, no pews or kneelers—just intense fervor reflected in their eyes and the bare floor beneath their knees.

No one ever leaves anyone else out of the Sign of Peace. From the senior officer to the lowest enlisted Marine, embraces are exchanged, and sincere wishes of peace are authentic and heartfelt! Holy Communion! I have never experienced communion like that among men who know that this could be their last! The Mass is brief but its effects are enduring.

. . . We still have one more Forward Operating Base that we are scheduled to visit for Mass. . . . When we arrive, more Marines than at any other stop that day gather for Mass. Several of the non-Catholics ask permission to join us so that they too can pray for their brothers. In the dimly lighted room, light begins to grow in the eyes of those who gather, and the intensity of the responses echo in the hall beyond us. In this moment, the Marine Corps motto, *Semper Fidelis* (Always Faithful), is incarnated in these men who gather around a simple table for this most sacred of Meals.

—**John Gayton,** adapted from "One Day in the Life of a Priest in Iraq," July 17, 2007

Reflect!

1. "Have you ever thought how you would prepare yourself to receive Our Lord if you could go to Communion only once in your life?" wrote St. Josemaría Escrivá. "We must be thankful to God that he makes it so easy for us to come to him: but we should show our gratitude by preparing ourselves to receive him very well" (*The Forge*).

   Consider how you come to the table of the Lord. Do you approach the altar with respect and receive the sacrament with reverence? Is your heart focused on Jesus, or are your thoughts scattered and distracted? Do you honor Jesus by your demeanor and dress? How can you prepare yourself to participate at Mass and receive Christ's body and blood in a more meaningful way?

2. Reflect on the following Scripture passages to deepen your understanding of the Eucharist:

   > The LORD said to Moses and Aaron in the land of Egypt:
   > ... Tell the whole congregation of Israel that on the tenth of this month they are to take a lamb for each family, a lamb for each household. If a household is too small for a whole lamb, it shall join its closest neighbor in obtaining one; the

lamb shall be divided in proportion to the number of people who eat of it. Your lamb shall be without blemish, a year-old male; you may take it from the sheep or from the goats. You shall keep it until the fourteenth day of this month; then the whole assembled congregation of Israel shall slaughter it at twilight. They shall take some of the blood and put it on the two doorposts and the lintel of the houses in which they eat it. They shall eat the lamb that same night; they shall eat it roasted over the fire with unleavened bread and bitter herbs. . . . This is how you shall eat it: your loins girded, your sandals on your feet, and your staff in your hand; and you shall eat it hurriedly. It is the passover of the LORD. For I will pass through the land of Egypt that night, and I will strike down every firstborn in the land of Egypt, both human beings and animals; on all the gods of Egypt I will execute judgments: I am the LORD. The blood shall be a sign for you on the houses where you live: when I see the blood, I will pass over you, and no plague shall destroy you when I strike the land of Egypt.

—Exodus 12:1, 3-8, 11-13

Jesus said to [the crowd who followed him after the multiplication of the loaves and fish], "I am the bread of life. Whoever comes to me will never be hungry, and whoever believes in me will never be thirsty. . . . I am the living bread that came down from heaven. Whoever eats of this bread will live forever; and the bread that I will give for the life of the world is my flesh."

The Jews then disputed among themselves, saying, "How can this man give us his flesh to eat?" So Jesus said to them, "Very truly I tell you, unless you eat the flesh of the Son of Man and drink his blood, you have no life in you. Those who eat my flesh and drink my blood have eternal life, and I will raise them up on the last day; for my flesh is true food and my blood is true drink. Those who eat my flesh and drink my blood abide in me, and I in them."

—John 6:35, 51-56

For our paschal lamb, Christ, has been sacrificed. Therefore, let us celebrate the festival, not with the old yeast, the yeast of malice and evil, but with the unleavened bread of sincerity and truth.

—1 Corinthians 5:7-8

The cup of blessing that we bless, is it not a sharing in the blood of Christ? The bread that we break, is it not a sharing in the body of Christ? Because there is one bread, we who are many are one body, for we all partake of the one bread.

—1 Corinthians 10:16-17

▶ In the Spotlight
A Pledge of Love

Having loved his own who were in the world, he loved them to the end (John 13:1). The love of friends increases at the time of death, when they are at the point of being separated from those they love. It is then they try more than ever, by some pledge of affection, to show the love they bear toward one another. Similarly, Jesus, during his whole life, gave us signs of his affection, but when he came near the hour of his death, he wished to give us a special proof of his love. What greater proof could this loving Lord show us than by giving his blood and his life for each of us? And not content with this, he left this very same body, sacrificed for us upon the cross, to be our food, so that the one who receives it would be wholly united to him, and that love should mutually increase.

—St. Alphonsus Liguori

Act!

St. Thomas Aquinas was known for his deep devotion to the Eucharist. When you attend Mass this week, pray this prayer written by him to help you prepare to receive Communion:

Almighty and ever-living God, I approach the sacrament of your only-begotten Son, our Lord Jesus Christ. I come sick to the doctor of life, unclean to the fountain of mercy, blind to the radiance of eternal light, and poor and needy to the Lord of heaven and earth. Lord, in your great generosity, heal my sickness, wash away my defilement, enlighten my blindness, enrich my poverty, and clothe my nakedness. May I receive the bread of angels, the King of kings and Lord of lords, with humble reverence, with the purity and faith, the repentance and love, and the determined purpose that will help to bring me to salvation. May I receive the sacrament of the Lord's Body and Blood, and its reality and power.

Kind God, may I receive the Body of your only-begotten Son, our Lord Jesus Christ, born from the womb of the Virgin Mary, and so be received into his mystical body and numbered among his members.

Loving Father, as on my earthly pilgrimage I now receive your beloved Son under the veil of a sacrament, may I one day see him face to face in glory, who lives and reigns with you forever. Amen.

▶ In the Spotlight
An Act of Thanksgiving

What is this sacrament called?. . . Eucharist, because it is an action of thanksgiving to God. The Greek words *eucharistein* [Luke 22:19; 1 Corinthians 11:24] and *eulogein* [Matthew 26:26; Mark 14:22] recall the Jewish blessings that proclaim—especially during a meal—God's works: creation, redemption, and sanctification.
—*Catechism of the Catholic Church,* 1328

The Word Incarnate is always there for us in the Eucharist. . . . When you receive him, you are like the Virgin Mary during the months she carried her child. You truly carry Christ within you and want to be absorbed in profound thanksgiving.
—**Père Jacques (Lucien-Louis Bunel)**

At every Mass we remember and relive the first sentiment expressed by Jesus as he broke the bread: that of *thanksgiving.* Gratitude is the disposition which lies at the root of the very word "Eucharist."
—**Pope John Paul II**

Union with Christ, to which the sacrament itself is directed, is not to be limited to the duration of the celebration of the Eucharist; it is to be prolonged into the entire Christian life, in such a way that the Christian faithful, contemplating unceasingly the gift they have received, may make their life a continual thanksgiving under the guidance of the Holy Spirit and may produce fruits of greater charity.
—*Instruction of the Sacred Congregation of Rites on the Worship of the Holy Eucharist*

Love's
Surrender

Mark 14:32-42

³² They went to a place called Gethsemane; and he said to his disciples, "Sit here while I pray." ³³He took with him Peter and James and John, and began to be distressed and agitated. ³⁴And he said to them, "I am deeply grieved, even to death; remain here, and keep awake." ³⁵And going a little farther, he threw himself on the ground and prayed that, if it were possible, the hour might pass from him. ³⁶He said, "Abba, Father, for you all things are possible; remove this cup from me; yet, not what I want, but what you want." ³⁷He came and found them sleeping; and he said to Peter, "Simon, are you asleep? Could you not keep awake one hour? ³⁸Keep awake and pray that you may not come into the time of trial; the spirit indeed is willing, but the flesh is weak." ³⁹And again he went away and prayed, saying the same words. ⁴⁰And once more he came and found them sleeping, for their eyes were very heavy; and they did not know what to say to him. ⁴¹He came a third time and said to them, "Are you still sleeping and taking your rest? Enough! The hour has come; the Son of Man is betrayed into the hands of sinners. ⁴²Get up, let us be going. See, my betrayer is at hand."
(See also Matthew 26:36-46; Luke 22:39-46.)

> In childlike trust Jesus surrendered His will to God. This was the weapon with which He defeated the prince of death and emerged from the battle as Victor.
> —Basilea Schlink, *The Holy Places Today*

After the Last Supper, Jesus withdrew with his disciples to the Mount of Olives to pray, knowing that in a few hours his mission and God's plan of salvation would be fulfilled by his passion and death. Earlier Peter, James, and John had been privileged to witness Jesus' glory at his transfiguration (see Matthew 17:1-13; Mark 9:2-13; Luke 9:28-36), perhaps to strengthen their faith so that they would be prepared to now witness his harrowing anguish in Gethsemane. But like Job's three friends Eliphaz, Bildad, and Zophar, who provided little comfort for Job because they couldn't grasp the "why" of his suffering, Peter and the sons of Zebedee gave Jesus no consolation during his hours of agony. Rather, they fell asleep as they had before on the mount of the transfiguration, this time overcome and fatigued by their grief (see Luke 9:32; 22:45).

Jesus urged his companions to stay awake and pray not to come into the time of trial (see Mark 14:38a), yet they failed to be vigilant—and thus they later lacked strength when tested and fled. Scripture scholar George Montague notes that when Jesus addressed the drowsy Peter, he used the apostle's "old pre-Christian name [Simon], evoking his human weakness." Jesus was saddened by his friends' failure but not surprised. Sharing in our humanness, he understood the weakness of the flesh even when the spirit is willing (see 14:38b).

Jesus' experience in Gethsemane was a critical point in his determination to hold fast to his call. In ancient times, the Greek word *agonia* was a technical term used to describe the sweat athletes produced as they did "warm-up" exercises to loosen up and ready their muscles for competing in the Olympic games. Seen in this light, Jesus' agony in the garden was a warm-up for his coming passion and crucifixion.

When, at the outset of his public ministry, Jesus had resisted Satan's attempts to deter him from his mission, the devil had "departed from him until an opportune time" (Luke 4:13). Now Jesus entered into a battle that would ultimately deliver all humankind from the power of

Satan. It would be a costly battle. Jesus would have to bear not only physical tortures and suffering but also "our sins in his body on the cross" (1 Peter 2:24). He would experience in his humanity a sense of abandonment by the Father (see Matthew 27:46). So great was this battle that, St. Luke mysteriously tells us, bloody sweat fell from him as he prayed. Yet, he had not been abandoned by his Father. Just as Jesus had been ministered to by angels after his encounter with Satan in the wilderness, an angel came to strengthen him (see Luke 22:43-44; Matthew 4:11; Mark 1:13).

Jesus wrestled with human dread of his impending torments, yet he submitted to the Father's will without any word of mistrust or rebellion: "Abba, Father, for you all things are possible; remove this cup from me; yet, not what I want, but what you want" (Mark 14:36). As Benedictine Sister Maria Boulding has observed:

Jesus won through those fearsome hours in Gethsemane, clinging to his knowledge of the Father's love for him and for all humankind.

Gethsemane was the death-struggle between all that was less than his vocation, yet still had power to attract him, and the purer, freer will in him that could be content with nothing less than abandonment to the utter mysteriousness of the Father's love. He died in this abandonment, believing in the love of the Father who delivered him to death and seemed to be silent. His act of surrender as he said, "Father, into thy hands I commit my spirit" was the breakthrough, the leap beyond all limitations; such obedient love could be vindicated only on the other side of death. St. Paul says that Christ was obedient unto death, but this inevitably meant obedient unto life: the unlimited life, love, freedom and joy of his resurrection. (*Prayer: Our Journey Home*)

Jesus won through those fearsome hours in Gethsemane, clinging to his knowledge of the Father's love for him and for all humankind. Readied by his firm acceptance of God's will, he went forward with peaceful dignity to receive Judas' traitorous kiss and meet his captors (see Mark 14:42-46).

Understand!

1. Explain the role of Peter, James, and John in Gethsemane. Why, in your opinion, did Jesus want them to remain close by and awake while he prayed? What adjectives would you choose to describe the apostles in this scene?

_____

_____

_____

_____

_____

_____

_____

2. What lesson(s) was Jesus attempting to teach Peter, James, and John through their experience in Gethsemane? What do you think the three learned about themselves?

_____

_____

_____

_____

_____

_____

_____

3. What words and phrases does Mark use to describe Jesus' physical and emotional state in Gethsemane? How are Jesus' two natures—the divine and the human—reflected in his prayer to the Father? How would you characterize Jesus' mind-set as expressed in his prayer?

_____

_____

_____

_____

_____

_____

4. In what way(s) are Adam and Eve's initial relationship with God in the garden of Eden and Jesus' relationship with his Father as portrayed in the garden of Gethsemane similar? What were the consequences of Adam and Eve's disobedience in Eden? What are the consequences of Jesus' resolution in Gethsemane?

_____

_____

_____

_____

_____

_____

5. During his agony in Gethsemane, do you think Jesus was struggling with himself? With Satan? With his Father? Explain your thoughts and insights.

_____

_____

_____

_____

_____

_____

▶ In the Spotlight
Contemporary Voices

There is a clear similarity between the prayer that Jesus gave his disciples and the one he prays to the Father in Gethsemane. In fact, he left us *his* prayer.

Jesus' prayer begins, as the Our Father does, with the cry, "Abba, Father" (Mark 14:36), or "my Father" (Matthew 26:39). It continues, like the Our Father, by asking that his will be done. He asks that the cup would pass from him, just as we ask in the Our Father to be "delivered from evil." He tells his disciples that they should pray not to yield to temptation, and he has us conclude the Our Father with the words, "Lead us not into temptation."

What comfort, in the hours of trial and darkness, to know that the Holy Spirit continues in us Jesus' prayer at Gethsemane, that the "sighs too deep for words" (Romans 8:26) with which the Spirit intercedes for us at those times reach the Father mixed together with the "prayers and supplications, with loud cries and tears" (Hebrews 5:7) that the Son lifted up to him when "his hour" had come!

—**Raniero Cantalamessa**, *Remember Jesus Christ*

Grow!

1. When have you been tempted, like Peter, James, and John, to "fall asleep," turning a blind eye to someone who is in distress or struggling to follow God's will? What attitudes (such as complacency, reluctance to get involved, feelings of inadequacy) might have held you back? What would help you to be more open to offering support in the future?

_____

_____

_____

_____

_____

_____

_____

2. Recall a time when it required great effort for you to accept God's will. Why was acceptance difficult for you? Fear of what God was asking of you? Reluctance to give up your own desires or plans? What was your prayer like then? What did you learn about yourself through this experience?

_____

_____

_____

_____

_____

_____

3. Do you address God as "Abba, Father" (Mark 14:36) as freely—
and as honestly—as Jesus did? What have you learned from the
way Jesus prayed in Gethsemane?

_____

_____

_____

_____

_____

_____

_____

4. To what specific area of your life do Jesus' words "the spirit indeed
is willing, but the flesh is weak" (Mark 14:38) apply right now?
What impact does knowing that Jesus understands your weakness have on you? Recast Jesus' prayer in Gethsemane in your
own words to help you surrender this area to God.

_____

_____

_____

_____

_____

_____

5. What are some dangers to your spiritual wellbeing and relationship with the Lord that you should be vigilant against? How might
Jesus' admonition "Keep awake and pray that you may not come
into the time of trial" (Mark 14:38) help you?

_____

_____

_____

_____

_____

▶ In the Spotlight
The Garden of Gethsemane

The garden of Gethsemane lies east of Jerusalem, beyond the Kidron Valley and at the foot of the Mount of Olives. The name "Gethsemane" is derived from the Hebrew word *Gat-shemanin*, meaning "oil press." Most likely, a press for extracting oil from olives was located in what may have been the garden of a private estate. Jesus and his apostles occasionally used the site as a place of retreat (see John 18:2). Nearby is a small cave, traditionally called the Grotto of Betrayal, where the disciples could have been resting when Judas led the band of Roman soldiers to Gethsemane to arrest Jesus.

Scripture scholars speculate that Gethsemane may have been owned by the family of Mark. The young man wearing a linen cloth who fled at Jesus' arrest was possibly the Evangelist's subtle reference to himself (see Mark 14:51-52), and his nighttime presence in the garden would be logically accounted for if the property belonged to his family.

On the traditional site, visited by millions of pilgrims over the centuries, are olive trees that are estimated to date from the seventh century. The Jewish historian Josephus Flavius noted the destruction of the olive trees on the Mount of Olives by the Roman army of Titus during the siege of Jerusalem in A.D. 68–70. Today the grove of olive trees is enclosed by a stone wall and cared for by the Franciscans. Next to the garden is the Church of the Nations, built in the early twentieth century over the ruins of Byzantine and crusader churches. Within it is preserved the traditional "Rock of Agony," recalling Jesus' anguished prayer.

The garden of Gethsemane where Jesus, the "New Adam," prevailed over temptation and embraced God's will, stands in contrast to the garden of Eden where Adam and Eve were tempted by Satan and disobeyed God.

Reflect!

1. Reflect on the Church's practice of inviting us, at the close of the liturgy on Holy Thursday evening, to remain in adoration of the Blessed Sacrament. We are urged to keep watch there, "reliving Jesus' agony in Gethsemane. . . . On this holy night of Gethsemane, let us be vigilant, not wanting to leave the Lord on his own at this time" (Pope Benedict XVI).

   Spend some special time with the Lord in prayer this week, either at home or in church before the Blessed Sacrament, reliving with him his agony in Gethsemane.

2. Reflect on the following Scripture passages to enhance your appreciation of the totality of Jesus' obedience to his Father:

   > Jesus said to [his disciples], "My food is to do the will of him who sent me and to complete his work."
   > —John 4:34

   > [Jesus said:] "For this reason the Father loves me, because I lay down my life in order to take it up again. No one takes it from me, but I lay it down of my own accord. I have power to lay it down, and I have power to take it up again. I have received this command from my Father."
   > —John 10:17-18

   > Though he was in the form of God,
   >   [he] did not regard equality with God
   >   as something to be exploited,
   > but emptied himself,
   >   taking the form of a slave,
   >   being born in human likeness.

And being found in human form,
   he humbled himself
   and became obedient to the point of death—
   even death on a cross.

—Philippians 2:6-8

In the days of his flesh, Jesus offered up prayers and supplications, with loud cries and tears, to the one who was able to save him from death, and he was heard because of his reverent submission. Although he was a Son, he learned obedience through what he suffered; and having been made perfect, he became the source of eternal salvation for all who obey him, having been designated by God a high priest according to the order of Melchizedek.

—Hebrews 5:7-10

▶ In the Spotlight
From the *Catechism of the Catholic Church*

The cup of the New Covenant, which Jesus anticipated when he offered himself at the Last Supper, is afterwards accepted by him from his Father's hands in his agony in the garden at Gethsemani, making himself "obedient unto death." Jesus prays: "My Father, if it be possible, let this cup pass from me. . . ." Thus he expresses the horror that death represented for his human nature. Like ours, his human nature is destined for eternal life; but unlike ours, it is perfectly exempt from sin, the cause of death. Above all, his human nature has been assumed by the divine person of the "Author of life," the "Living One." By accepting in his human will that the Father's will be done, he accepts his death as redemptive, for "he himself bore our sins in his body on the tree." (612)

Act!

Raniero Cantalamessa noted in the Lenten meditations he presented to Pope Benedict XVI and the papal household in 2006:

> How many hidden Gethsemanes there are in the world, perhaps under our own roofs, or next door, or at the desk next to ours at the office! Let us find someone like this during this Lent and draw close to that person where they are. May Jesus not have to say about us, his members,
>
> > I looked for pity, but there was none;
> > and for comforters, but I found none.
> > (Psalm 69:20)
>
> On the contrary, may Jesus be able to speak in our hearts the word that repays us for everything: "You did it to me" (Matthew 25:40).

This week, reach out and encourage someone you know who is in a "hidden Gethsemane"—perhaps facing the loss of a job, a diagnosis of a serious illness, or the death of a loved one. Offer support, strength, and comfort to this person by your presence as well as by your intercessory prayer.

▶ In the Spotlight
"His Sweat Became Like Great Drops of Blood"

The Evangelist Luke, a physician, noted that in his intense agony, Jesus' sweat became bloody (see Luke 22:44). This is a rare but actual physiological phenomenon known as hematidrosis. In situations of great anxiety, acute fear, or intense emotional stress and pressure, the tiny capillaries in and surrounding the sweat glands constrict and dilate. If these capillaries rupture, the result is an excretion of blood into the sweat glands and the body's perspiration is colored with droplets of blood. In hematidrosis, the blood loss is usually negligible, but the skin becomes very tender, sensitive, and fragile. Thus, the first drops of Jesus' blood were shed and the physical pains of his passion began with his agony in Gethsemane, even before his scourging and crucifixion.

"I Am"

John 18:1-9, 12-14

¹ [Jesus] went out with his disciples across the Kidron valley to a place where there was a garden, which he and his disciples entered. ²Now Judas, who betrayed him, also knew the place, because Jesus often met there with his disciples. ³So Judas brought a detachment of soldiers together with police from the chief priests and the Pharisees, and they came there with lanterns and torches and weapons. ⁴Then Jesus, knowing all that was to happen to him, came forward and asked them, "Whom are you looking for?"

> Jesus unleashes the power of the divine name, "I AM," simply by uttering it.
> —*Ignatius Catholic Study Bible: The Gospel of John*

⁵They answered, "Jesus of Nazareth." Jesus replied, "I am he." Judas, who betrayed him, was standing with them. ⁶When Jesus said to them, "I am he," they stepped back and fell to the ground. ⁷Again he asked them, "Whom are you looking for?" And they said, "Jesus of Nazareth." ⁸Jesus answered, "I told you that I am he. So if you are looking for me, let these men go." ⁹This was to fulfill the word that he had spoken, "I did not lose a single one of those whom you gave me."

¹² So the soldiers, their officer, and the Jewish police arrested Jesus and bound him. ¹³First they took him to Annas, who was the father-in-law of Caiaphas, the high priest that year. ¹⁴Caiaphas was the one who had advised the Jews that it was better to have one person die for the people.

(See also Matthew 26:47-57; Mark 14:43-50, 53; Luke 22:47-54.)

Mark 14:55-64; 15:1

^{14:55} Now the chief priests and the whole council were looking for testimony against Jesus to put him to death; but they found none. ⁵⁶For many gave false testimony against him, and their testimony did not agree. ⁵⁷Some stood up and gave false testimony against him, saying, ⁵⁸"We heard him say, 'I will destroy this temple that is made with hands, and in three days I will build another, not made with hands.'" ⁵⁹But even on this point their testimony did not agree. ⁶⁰Then the high priest stood up before them and asked Jesus, "Have you no answer? What is it that they testify against you?" ⁶¹But he was silent and did not answer. Again the high priest asked him, "Are you the Messiah, the Son of the Blessed One?" ⁶²Jesus said, "I am; and

'you will see the Son of Man
seated at the right hand of the Power,'
and 'coming with the clouds of heaven.'"

⁶³Then the high priest tore his clothes and said, "Why do we still need witnesses? ⁶⁴You have heard his blasphemy! What is your decision?" All of them condemned him as deserving death. . . .

^{15:1}As soon as it was morning, the chief priests held a consultation with the elders and scribes and the whole council. They bound Jesus, led him away, and handed him over to Pilate.
(See also Matthew 26:59-66; 27:1-2; Luke 22:66-71; 23:1; John 18:12-14, 19-24.)

Unlike the other gospel writers, John did not describe Jesus' anguished prayer in Gethsemane. Nonetheless, earlier in this gospel, Jesus' struggle with his impending death, and his assent to his Father's plan of salvation, are recounted by the Evangelist: "Now my soul is troubled. And what should I say—'Father, save me from this hour'? No, it is for this reason that I have come to this hour. Father, glorify your name" (John 12:27-28; see also 10:18). Now we encounter Jesus in the garden, ready to go forward with resolve and spiritual and moral strength to meet Judas and his captors. As if to emphasize this treacherous breach of friendship, John notes that Judas knew where to find Jesus—as one of the apostles, the betrayer had often been in Gethsemane with Jesus (see 18:2).

The soldiers who came to arrest Jesus were armed, yet Jesus is the one who dominates the scene. With calm authority—even majesty—he confronted the guards first, asking "Whom are you looking for?" To their reply, "Jesus the Nazorean," he responded with the deeper truth of his divinity, "I AM" (John 18:3-5, New American Bible).

When God told Moses his "personal" name "I AM" in the encounter in the burning bush (see Exodus 3:13-14), he was revealing his divine Person, his nature and his character. The Hebrew phrase *'ehyeh 'asher 'ehyeh* is usually translated as "I AM WHO I AM," expressing absolute being, or as "I will cause to be what I will cause to be," which includes a sense of causality, that is, the principle of cause and effect. Yet no translation is entirely satisfactory: "This divine name is mysterious just as God is mystery. It is at once a name revealed and something like the refusal of a name, and hence it better expresses God as what he is—infinitely above everything that we can understand" (*Catechism of the Catholic Church*, 206). By stating this name as his own, Jesus was clearly identifying himself as God.

Even as Jesus gave himself over voluntarily to his passion, he cared for his disciples. Earlier he had declared that none of his own would be lost except Judas (see John 6:39; 17:12). Although this was primarily an assurance that they would be protected from eternal punishment, Jesus was also concerned for his followers' immediate safety. Like a shepherd protecting his flock from wolves and brigands (see 10:7-13), Jesus negotiated their release: "If you are looking for me, let these men go" (18:8). Matthew (26:56) and Mark (14:50) note that the disciples fled when Jesus was arrested—most likely this was after Jesus had made sure that they would not be seized by the soldiers.

The Jewish authorities had long sought to do away with Jesus (see Matthew 26:3-5; Mark 14:1-2; Luke 22:1-2; John 7:1, 30, 32; 11:57). Now Jesus was brought captive before the chief priests and the Jewish council known as the Sanhedrin in an irregular nighttime meeting, probably to avoid rousing the opposition of those who supported the popular rabbi. The hearing initially focused on charges regarding what Jesus had said about the Temple. Jesus' disruption of the commerce in the Temple precincts (see John 2:15-18) and his allusion to the Temple's destruction (see 2:19-21) were a threat to the authorities who controlled and profited from the enterprise of the Temple. Jesus did not respond to the conflicting witnesses and misinterpretation of his words; his silence recalls Isaiah's prophecy: "Like a lamb that is led to the slaughter, / and like a sheep that before its shearers is silent, / so he did not open his mouth" (53:7).

When he failed to obtain concurring testimony against Jesus, Caiaphas tried to back Jesus into a corner where he would convict himself with his own words. Pressing on to the crux of the matter, the high priest asked him directly, "Are you the Messiah, the Son of the Blessed One?" (Mark 14:61). To deny being the Christ would contradict all that Jesus had said and done, but if he said yes, his answer would be interpreted as blasphemy, an insult to God's name, and a capital crime, punishable by death (see Leviticus 24:16).

Jesus' reply was unhesitating and unambiguous: "I am" (Mark 14:62). Ironically, it was at this climatic moment, when he seemed most powerless, that Jesus' true identity became apparent: he was not a political messiah-king who had come to overthrow Israel's oppressors but Yahweh's "Suffering Servant" (see Isaiah 52:13–53:12). And it is this suffering Messiah—the "Son of Man" and our redeemer—who now sits at the right hand of God and whose kingdom will last forever (see Mark 14:62; Daniel 7:13-14).

Understand!

1. What human and divine qualities did Jesus exhibit at his arrest? How, and why, are his divine identity and authority made so evident then? What light does John 10:17-18 shed on Jesus' control of the events in Gethsemane?

_____

_____

_____

_____

_____

_____

_____

2. Read Matthew 26:14-16; Luke 22:3-6; and John 6:60-71, 12:4-6 for insight into Judas and his actions. Why do you think he betrayed Jesus? What do Jesus' sorrow over Judas at the Last Supper (see John 13:21-30) and his calling Judas "friend" in Gethsemane (see Matthew 26:48-50) suggest to you about Jesus' feelings for this disciple?

_____

_____

_____

_____

3. Why did the Jewish leaders, and Caiaphas in particular, seek to do away with Jesus (see John 6:25-32; 9:13-34; 11:45-53)? What was confusing and false about the testimony against Jesus given in Mark 14:56-59? Jesus referred to himself as the true temple of God. In what way(s) is Jesus God's temple (see John 2:19-21)?

_____

_____

_____

_____

_____

_____

_____

4. Why do you think Jesus remained silent before the Jewish council? What effect did Jesus' silence have on Caiaphas? Why, in your opinion, did Jesus finally acknowledge his identity?

_____

_____

_____

_____

_____

_____

5. What do you understand by Jesus' description of himself in Mark 14:62 (see also Daniel 7:13-14)? Did the high priest actually have legal grounds on which to sentence Jesus? Explain.

_____

_____

_____

_____

_____

_____

▶ In the Spotlight
Contemporary Voices

The central word in the story of Jesus' arrest is one I never thought much about. It is "to be handed over." That is what happened in Gethsemane. Jesus was handed over. Some translations say that Jesus was "betrayed," but the Greek says he was "handed over." Judas handed Jesus over (see Mark 14:10). But the remarkable thing is that the same word is used not only for Judas but also for God. God did not spare Jesus, but handed him over to benefit us all (see Romans 8:32).

So this word, "to be handed over," plays a central role in the life of Jesus. Indeed, this drama of being handed over divides the life of Jesus radically in two. The first part of Jesus' life is filled with activity. Jesus takes all sorts of initiatives. He speaks; he preaches; he heals; he travels. But immediately after Jesus is handed over, he becomes the one to whom things are being done. He's being arrested; he's being led to the high priest; he's being taken before Pilate; he's being crowned with thorns; he's being nailed on a cross. Things are being done to him over which he has no control. That is the meaning of passion—being the recipient of other people's initiatives.

—**Henri Nouwen**, *Bread and Wine*

Grow!

1. What does God's name "I AM" mean to you personally? How are we able to have a personal relationship with God when he remains such a mystery to us?

   _____

   _____

   _____

   _____

   _____

   _____

2. Recall an instance when you were either deeply hurt by someone who failed you or betrayed by someone whom you loved and trusted. How did you deal with the hurt? How did the Lord help you to heal? Were you able to forgive?

   _____

   _____

   _____

   _____

   _____

   _____

3. Do you recognize any ways in which you have "betrayed" Jesus? If so, why or how? Because of fear or peer pressure? Out of self-interest and personal ambition? By failing to trust him or to live according to his commandments? Now ask the Lord for his forgiveness and the grace to amend your ways—remember, the Lord loves you and is merciful!

   _____

   _____

_____

_____

_____

_____

_____

_____

4. Do you think it is always right (or necessary) to defend yourself
   when wrongly accused? Why or why not? In your opinion, does
   silence express consent and agreement, or does it suggest a denial
   of guilt? Have you ever remained silent in the face of false accu-
   sation or slander and been vindicated? Explain.

_____

_____

_____

_____

_____

_____

5. What impresses you most strongly about Jesus' bearing in the scene
   of his arrest? In the scene before Caiaphas? What have you learned
   from Jesus' example? Currently are there any situations in your
   life where you need to put these lessons into practice?

_____

_____

_____

_____

_____

_____

▶ In the Spotlight
The Judas in Me

Forgive my betrayals, Lord:

Those countless times
when I've slighted you
and turned away at your approach;
denied any knowledge of you by my nervous silence,
too embarrassed to stand up or speak for you;
or feigned false ignorance and bland disinterest,
failing to admit my allegiance to you
and all my heart's devotion.

Forgive the Judas in me
(and the Peter, too)
when I fall short
and save me from despair
as I shed now these tears of shame and sorrow
for my disloyalties to you.
—**Jeanne Kun,** *My Lord and My God! A Scriptural Journey with the Followers of Jesus*

The horror of Judas is not that he was unlike the other disciples but that he was just like them. He enjoyed all their advantages, above all the personal closeness to Jesus. Yet he could choose to deny him.

We are being asked here to examine not the problem of Judas and his sin but the problem of our own: why do we betray, and walk away?
—**Wendy Beckett,** *Sister Wendy's Nativity*

Reflect!

1. Reflect on 1 John 2:1-2: "If anyone does sin, we have an advocate with the Father, Jesus Christ the righteous; and he is the atoning sacrifice for our sins, and not for ours only but also for the sins of the whole world."

   Make an examination of conscience. Then express to God your sorrow for your sins in an act of contrition. If you need to offer forgiveness or seek forgiveness from anyone, ask Jesus for his help to do this. If possible, receive the Sacrament of Reconciliation this week.

2. Reflect on the following passages to deepen your understanding and appreciation of what it means that Jesus was condemned to death for our sake:

   > By a perversion of justice he was taken away.
   >   Who could have imagined his future?
   > For he was cut off from the land of the living,
   >   stricken for the transgression of my people.
   > They made his grave with the wicked
   >   and his tomb with the rich,
   > although he had done no violence,
   >   and there was no deceit in his mouth.
   >
   > Therefore I will allot him a portion with the great,
   >   and he shall divide the spoil with the strong;
   > because he poured out himself to death,
   >   and was numbered with the transgressors;
   > yet he bore the sin of many,
   >   and made intercession for the transgressors.
   >   —Isaiah 53:8-9, 12

The free gift is not like the trespass. For if the many died through the one man's [Adam's] trespass, much more surely have the grace of God and the free gift in the grace of the one man, Jesus Christ, abounded for the many. And the free gift is not like the effect of the one man's sin. For the judgment following one trespass brought condemnation, but the free gift following many trespasses brings justification. If, because of the one man's trespass, death exercised dominion through that one, much more surely will those who receive the abundance of grace and the free gift of righteousness exercise dominion in life through the one man, Jesus Christ.

Therefore just as one man's trespass led to condemnation for all, so one man's act of righteousness leads to justification and life for all. For just as by the one man's disobedience the many were made sinners, so by the one man's obedience the many will be made righteous. But law came in, with the result that the trespass multiplied; but where sin increased, grace abounded all the more, so that, just as sin exercised dominion in death, so grace might also exercise dominion through justification leading to eternal life through Jesus Christ our Lord.

—Romans 5:15-21

There is therefore now no condemnation for those who are in Christ Jesus. For the law of the Spirit of life in Christ Jesus has set you free from the law of sin and of death. For God has done what the law, weakened by the flesh, could not do: by sending his own Son in the likeness of sinful flesh, and to deal with sin, he condemned sin in the flesh, so that the just requirement of the law might be fulfilled in us, who walk not according to the flesh but according to the Spirit. . . . If the Spirit of him who raised Jesus from the dead dwells in you, he who raised Christ from

the dead will give life to your mortal bodies also through
his Spirit that dwells in you.

—Romans 8:1-4, 11

▶ In the Spotlight
On Trial for the Sake of Christ

*Théophane Vénard (b. 1829), a French priest of the Paris Foreign
Missionary Society, was arrested, tried, and sentenced to death
for his evangelistic activities in Annam (present-day Vietnam).
This dialogue is from the description of his trial that Vénard
was able to write in a letter to his family during his imprison-
ment and secretly pass to a fellow priest:*

"Great mandarin! I do not fear death. I have come here to
preach the true religion. I am guilty of no crime which deserves
death. But if the Annamites kill me, I shall shed my blood with
great joy for them."

"Have you any spite or ill will against the man who betrayed
you and took you prisoner?"

"None at all. The Christian religion forbids us to entertain
anger, and teaches us to love those who hate us." . . .

"Trample the Cross under foot, then, and you shall not be
put to death."

"How! I have preached the religion of the Cross all my life
until this day, and do you expect me to adjure it now? I do not
esteem so highly the pleasures of this life as to be willing to buy
the preservation of it by apostasy."

*Théophane Vénard was beheaded in 1861 and canonized with
116 other nineteenth-century martyrs of Vietnam by Pope John
Paul II in 1988. Today, in spite of repression by the Communist
government, the Vietnamese Church is growing and continues
to give bold witness to the faith of its martyrs.*

Act!

As a young girl, St. Thérèse of Lisieux heard that a notorious murderer, Henri Pranzini, had been sentenced to death. She felt moved to pray for his eternal salvation, and even boldly asked God to give her a sign of the condemned man's repentance. The day after his execution, Thérèse learned from a newspaper account that on the scaffold, Pranzini had taken hold of the crucifix held out to him by a priest and kissed Christ's wounds three times. Thérèse considered Pranzini the "first child" of her ardent thirst and prayers for the conversion of sinners.

Today millions of men and women are in prisons around the world, some justly incarcerated for crimes they committed, others unjustly condemned—as Jesus was—by oppressive governments, unscrupulous judges, or false testimony. Countless others are imprisoned for their faith.

Take at least one of the following actions:

• Intercede for those—both the guilty and the innocent—who are in state prisons, correctional institutions, or on death row, as well as for those who are persecuted or imprisoned for their faith.

• Find out about your local jail ministry and get involved (visiting those in prison is one of the corporal works of mercy: see Matthew 25:36, 39-40).

• Join a prison pen-pal program and write to a prison inmate.

• Donate to Partners in Evangelism Ministry to Prisoners, an outreach of The Word Among Us, Inc., that provides *The Word Among Us* magazine and other inspirational booklets free to Catholic prisoners (currently 45,000 prisoners in more than 1,000 institutions are being served by this ministry).

▶ In the Spotlight
The Sanhedrin

In the Jerusalem of Jesus' day, there was one principal assembly which served as the judicial supreme court and the legislative council. The Greek name for this council in both the New Testament and late Jewish writings is the Sanhedrin. According to the Mishnah, a third-century Jewish document, this council had 71 members and met in the Chamber of Hewn Stone on the grounds of the Temple complex. It made final decisions in legal disputes, judged the fitness of priests to serve in the Temple, and decided on additions to the Temple.

The Jerusalem council was presided over by the high priest, and was made up of high officials and the senior members of the powerful priestly and aristocratic families. One of their roles seems to have been mediation between the Roman Empire and the Jewish people. Its influence probably varied from one period to another, depending on the political strength of the high priest in office and the degree of freedom given to the Jewish assembly by the Roman governors. According to our modern terminology, it was both a religious and a secular council, since there was no distinction in ancient Jerusalem between religious laws and practices and political and social life.

The Gospels indicate that this council conducted the preliminary trial of Jesus. According to Matthew 26:59, "The chief priests and the whole council were looking for false testimony against Jesus so that they might put him to death." It seems that the high priest's strategy was to unite the various parties within the council in a unanimous condemnation of Jesus.

—Stephen Binz, "The Crowds and the Authorities in the Passion Narratives"

A Love
unto Death

John 19:13-22, 25-37

[13] [Pilate] brought Jesus outside and sat on the judge's bench at a place called The Stone Pavement, or in Hebrew Gabbatha. [14]Now it was the day of Preparation for the Passover; and it was about noon. He said to the Jews, "Here is your King!" [15]They cried out, "Away with him! Away with him! Crucify him!" Pilate asked them, "Shall I crucify your King?" The chief priests answered, "We have no king but the emperor." [16]Then he handed him over to them to be crucified.

So they took Jesus; [17]and carrying the cross by himself, he went out to what is called The Place of the Skull, which in Hebrew is called Golgotha. [18]There they crucified him, and with him two others, one on either side, with Jesus between them. [19]Pilate also had an inscription written and put on the cross. It read, "Jesus of Nazareth, the King of the Jews." [20]Many of the Jews read this inscription, because the place where Jesus was crucified was near the city; and it was written in Hebrew, in Latin, and in Greek. [21]Then the chief priests of the Jews said to Pilate, "Do not write, 'The King of the Jews,' but, 'This man said, I am King of the Jews.'" [22]Pilate answered, "What I have written I have written." . . .

[25] [S]tanding near the cross of Jesus were his mother, and his mother's sister, Mary the wife of Clopas, and Mary Magdalene. [26]When Jesus saw his mother and the disciple whom he loved standing beside her, he said to his mother, "Woman, here is your son." [27]Then he said to the disciple, "Here is your mother." And from that hour the disciple took her into his own home.

[28] After this, when Jesus knew that all was now finished, he said (in order to fulfill the scripture), "I am thirsty." [29]A jar full of

> On Golgotha Jesus' Heart was pierced by a lance as a sign of his total self-giving, of that sacrificial and saving love with which he "loved us to the end" (John 13:1), laying the foundation of the friendship between God and man.
>
> —Pope John Paul II

sour wine was standing there. So they put a sponge full of the wine on a branch of hyssop and held it to his mouth. ³⁰When Jesus had received the wine, he said, "It is finished." Then he bowed his head and gave up his spirit.

³¹ Since it was the day of Preparation, the Jews did not want the bodies left on the cross during the sabbath, especially because that sabbath was a day of great solemnity. So they asked Pilate to have the legs of the crucified men broken and the bodies removed. ³²Then the soldiers came and broke the legs of the first and of the other who had been crucified with him. ³³But when they came to Jesus and saw that he was already dead, they did not break his legs. ³⁴Instead, one of the soldiers pierced his side with a spear, and at once blood and water came out. ³⁵(He who saw this has testified so that you also may believe. His testimony is true, and he knows that he tells the truth.) ³⁶These things occurred so that the scripture might be fulfilled, "None of his bones shall be broken." ³⁷And again another passage of scripture says, "They will look on the one whom they have pierced."

(See Matthew 27:32-54; Mark 15:20b-39; Luke 23:26-49.)

Jesus' journey led from the house of Caiaphas to Pontius Pilate's official quarters in Jerusalem, most likely located in the Antonia Fortress (see John 18:28). It would be Jesus' last stopping place before Golgotha.

As the Roman governor of Judea, Pilate possessed the *jus gladii* (the "right of the sword"), the authority to order an execution. Although the Jewish religious leaders despised Pilate, they had to submit their case to him if they wanted Jesus to be sentenced to death; the Sanhedrin was under Roman jurisdiction and had no authority to impose capital punishment (see John 18:29-31).

Pilate repeatedly declared Jesus innocent of any crime. In fact, he tried several times to avoid condemning him; he even had Jesus scourged in an attempt to appease the Jewish leaders and win the crowd's sympathy (see Luke 23:13-16; John 18:28–19:12).

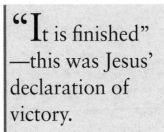

"It is finished" —this was Jesus' declaration of victory.

Nonetheless, the chief priests and elders were unyielding, and Pilate buckled under their pressure. Although Pilate knew Jesus had done nothing to deserve the death sentence, he lacked the courage and integrity to release him. When the Jews reminded Pilate that anyone who made himself a king was Caesar's rival, he acquiesced to the chief priests' demands in order to preserve crowd control and protect his political career from the emperor's displeasure (see John 19:12-16). Knowing that he was handing over an innocent man to quell an impending riot, Pilate tried to salve his conscience by symbolically washing his hands of responsibility for Jesus' death (see Matthew 27:24).

Mary remained steadfastly by Jesus as he hanged on the cross, demonstrating her solidarity with him and his mission. How terrible it must have been for her to see her son's agony; yet she would not leave him without the comfort of her maternal presence. And even in his suffering, Jesus thought of his mother, entrusting her to the beloved disciple's care. But first he directed Mary to extend her motherly care to John, thus creating a new spiritual family at Golgotha (see John 19:26-27). Mary's maternal role now has a universal dimension; her motherhood extends spiritually to all humanity.

Standing nearby, John was able to hear and record for us Jesus' last words from the cross: "It is finished" (John 19:30). In colloquial English, we might say, "I have done it!" This was a declaration of victory. "Jesus must have died in an ecstasy of joy, knowing that at last he had completed the work that he was born to accomplish" (Wendy Beckett, *Sister Wendy's Nativity*). Then he "gave up his spirit" (19:30), that is, handed himself over to the Father.

According to Jewish custom, the slaughter of the Passover lambs in the Temple—male lambs without blemish (see Exodus 12:5)—began at noon on the day of Preparation. And it was at that very hour that Pilate handed Jesus over to be crucified, even though he had found no fault in him (see John 19:14). While the blood of the paschal lambs was being poured out to commemorate the Israelites' deliverance from their bondage in Egypt, the blood of Jesus, the Lamb of God (see John 1:29), was being poured out on Golgotha to free us from the power of sin and Satan. And just as the bones of the Passover lambs were not broken (see Exodus 12:46; Numbers 9:12), neither were Jesus' legs broken, as was commonly done to hasten the death of a crucifixion victim (see John 19:32-33, 36; Psalm 34:20).

Finally, in his eyewitness account, John testifies that water and blood flowed from Jesus' side when a lance was thrust into his body (see John 19:34). Now we have access to an inexhaustible source of eternal life: we are cleansed and purified from our sins by the waters of baptism, and in the Eucharist we drink from the fountain that flows from the heart of our crucified Savior. The Church, born from Jesus' pierced side, is continually invigorated and renewed by these sacraments. And, as Pope Benedict XVI notes, it is by contemplating Christ's wounded heart that we become "sensitive to God's salvific will. It enables us to entrust ourselves to his saving and merciful love, and at the same time strengthens us in the desire to take part in his work of salvation, becoming his instruments."

Understand!

1. Why, in your opinion, was Pilate so adamant about the wording of the inscription placed on Jesus' cross (see John 19:19–22)? What does this suggest about Pilate's view of Jesus? About Pilate's feelings toward the chief priests? What does this incident add to your impressions of Pilate?

_____

_____

_____

_____

_____

_____

2. Choose several adjectives to characterize Jesus' relationship with his mother. Describe some of the human and natural dimensions of their relationship with each other. What qualities does Mary bring to her role as mother of the Church?

_____

_____

_____

_____

_____

_____

3. What similarities do you see between the Israelites' Passover deliverance from Egypt and Jesus' sacrifice on the cross at Golgotha? What differences?

_____

_____

_____

_____

_____

_____

_____

4. What is the significance of Jesus' words "It is finished" (John 19:30)? Read Ephesians 2:13-16 and Hebrews 9:11-15. What did Jesus accomplish by shedding his blood for us on the cross?

_____

_____

_____

_____

_____

_____

_____

5. Why is it so important that the Evangelist John was an eyewitness to the events of Jesus' life, ministry, and passion and so clearly stated this fact in his gospel (see John 19:35)? Read John 15:27 and 21:24 for more insight into the validity and significance of John's testimony.

_____

_____

_____

_____

_____

_____

▶ In the Spotlight
Jesus of Nazareth, the King of the Jews

Jesus was recognized and honored as the newborn king of the Jews by the gentile wise men who paid him homage at his birth (see Matthew 2:1-11), but the leaders of his own nation did not accept the truth of his kingship. When the chief priests and Sanhedrin brought Jesus before Pilate, they accused him of sedition and falsely claiming to be a king: "We found this man perverting our nation, forbidding us to pay taxes to the emperor, and saying that he himself is the Messiah, a king" (Luke 23:2). Ironically, it was the gentile Pilate who defied the Jewish elders and accorded the title "King of the Jews" to Jesus at his death (see John 19:19-22).

It was customary to write the crime of the accused on a placard that was then carried in front of him as he made his way to the place of execution, where it was either affixed to his cross or hung around his neck. The inscription that Pilate ordered to describe Jesus' "crime"—"Jesus of Nazareth, the King of the Jews" (John 19:19)—was written in Hebrew, the language of the Jews and their religion; in Latin, the language of the governing empire and its law; and in Greek, the language of culture. Thus, it universally proclaimed the truth of Jesus' divine kingship as he was "enthroned" on Golgotha. "The superscription is written and placed above, not below the cross," noted St. Ambrose, "because the government is upon his shoulders [Isaiah 9:6]. What is this government if not his eternal power and Godhead?. . . The superscription is fittingly above the cross, because although the Lord Jesus was on the cross, he shines above the cross with the majesty of a king."

Grow!

1. Like Pilate, have you ever yielded to fear, social or political pressure, or self-interest and made a wrong decision against your better judgment? Are you sometimes more concerned about personal advantage and what others think of you than with upholding God's teachings and values? What might you do to strengthen your resolve to choose rightly in the future?

   _____

   _____

   _____

   _____

   _____

   _____

   _____

2. Recall a time when you comforted and/or remained faithfully by someone dear to you when that person was in a time of deep distress or trial. What did this effort cost you? What enabled you to be steadfast? What have you learned from Mary's presence during Jesus' crucifixion that can help you support others in their difficulties or suffering?

   _____

   _____

   _____

   _____

   _____

   _____

   _____

3. What particular work or mission has God entrusted to you? How do you feel about carrying out this task? How has this changed your life? Ask the Holy Spirit to help you fulfill God's mission so that you will one day be able to say, as Jesus did, "It is finished."

_____

_____

_____

_____

_____

_____

_____

4. Which moment from John's account of the events on Golgotha moves you most profoundly? Why? What impact has Jesus' crucifixion had on you? How is the victory of the cross manifested in your life?

_____

_____

_____

_____

_____

_____

_____

5. In what way(s) do you acknowledge Jesus' kingship over you? What could you do to grow in loving Jesus more deeply? To respond more actively to his authority in your life?

_____

_____

_____

_____

_____

_____

▶ In the Spotlight
Mary at the Foot of the Cross

Only a consistency that lasts throughout the whole of life can be called faithfulness. Mary's *fiat* in the Annunciation finds its fullness in the silent *fiat* that she repeats at the foot of the cross.
—**Pope John Paul II**

Nor was Mary less than was befitting the mother of Christ. When the apostles fled, she stood before the cross and with reverent gaze beheld her Son's wounds, for she waited not for her child's death, but the world's salvation.
—**St. Ambrose**

Just as the Father gave us the great gift of his Son to be our Redeemer, so also the Son gives us the great gift of his Blessed Mother to be our Advocate. When he said to John at the foot of the Cross: "Behold your Mother!" he said it to him representing all Christians.
—**St. John of Ávila**

Reflect!

1. Reflect on this statement by St. Josemaría Escrivá:

John, the disciple whom Jesus loved, brought Mary into his home, into his life. Spiritual writers have seen these words of the Gospel as an invitation to all Christians to bring Mary into their lives. Mary certainly wants us to invoke her, to approach her confidently, to appeal to her as our mother, asking her to "show that you are our mother."

How do you express your relationship to Mary as your "spiritual mother"? In what ways can you more consciously bring Mary into your home and make a place for her in your life as the apostle John did?

2. Reflect on the following passages to enhance your understanding of the significance and power of Christ's death on the cross:

> Surely he has borne our infirmities
>   and carried our diseases;
> yet we accounted him stricken,
>   struck down by God, and afflicted.
> But he was wounded for our transgressions,
>   crushed for our iniquities;
> upon him was the punishment that made us whole,
>   and by his bruises we are healed.
> All we like sheep have gone astray;
>   we have all turned to our own way,
> and the LORD has laid on him
>   the iniquity of us all.
>
> —Isaiah 53:4-6

> When you were dead in trespasses and the uncircumcision of your flesh, God made you alive together with him, when he forgave us all our trespasses, erasing the record that stood against us with its legal demands. He set this aside, nailing it to the cross.
>
> —Colossians 2:13-14

Let us run with perseverance the race that is set before us, looking to Jesus the pioneer and perfecter of our faith, who for the sake of the joy that was set before him endured the cross, disregarding its shame, and has taken his seat at the right hand of the throne of God.

—Hebrews 12:1-2

Christ also suffered for you, leaving you an example, so that you should follow in his steps.
"He committed no sin,
    and no deceit was found in his mouth."
When he was abused, he did not return abuse; when he suffered, he did not threaten; but he entrusted himself to the one who judges justly. He himself bore our sins in his body on the cross, so that, free from sins, we might live for righteousness; by his wounds you have been healed.

—1 Peter 2:21-24

▶ In the Spotlight
Pontius Pilate

"Pontius" was a hereditary family name of Roman origin. The given name "Pilate" was probably derived from the Latin *pilatus*—a "pikeman" or person armed with a *pilum* or javelin. Pontius Pilate's wife was Claudia Procula, granddaughter of the emperor Augustus Caesar.

Pontius Pilate was appointed the Roman governor of Judea, Idumea, and Samaria in A.D. 26. He held the official title of prefect (military commander), but also performed the duties of a procurator (civil administrator). Apparently Pilate was an able administrator since he remained in office ten years, while the region had had four governors in the previous twenty years. But he was also a harsh and insensitive ruler who made himself unpopular with the Jewish people by bringing images of the Roman emperor into the Temple precincts in Jerusalem and by using money from the Temple treasury to pay for the construction of an aqueduct.

Pilate's headquarters were in Caesarea on the Mediterranean coast in the palace built by Herod the Great. Most of the soldiers under his command were stationed there, but others manned the Antonia Fortress, adjacent to the Temple in Jerusalem. During Passover, Pilate and his Caesarea troops went to Jerusalem to keep order among the pilgrims and crowds gathered for the feast. Pilate retained Caiaphas as the Jewish high priest during his whole term as governor, which suggests that the two men maintained a working relationship, most likely playing off one another's political interests and ambitions.

In A.D. 36 Pilate was removed as governor after his troops killed some Samaritans. Nothing certain is known of his later history. According to one tradition, he was executed by the emperor Nero. Another tradition holds that Pilate was exiled by the emperor Caligula to Gaul, where he committed suicide.

Act!

St. Teresa of Ávila experienced a fuller conversion and deepening of her prayer life after seeing an image that portrayed the wounded Christ. St. John of the Cross was frequently moved by depictions of scenes from Christ's life, and he taught that religious paintings should be prized because they point the heart toward the living image or mystery that they represent. As art historian Sr. Wendy Beckett points out, "Gazing upon sacred art is an exercise in prayer! The artists, by their very nature, and perhaps without even knowing it, teach us to pray!" (*In the Midst of Chaos, Peace*).

Kneel before a crucifix or sit quietly before a painting or icon depicting Jesus' passion. Allow the image to lead you into prayer. Tell

Jesus of your love for him and express your gratitude for his death on the cross.

▶ In the Spotlight
"I Have Done All You Gave Me to Do"

"It is consummated." These are our Lord's last words to his Father cited in St. John [19:30]. "I have done all you gave me to do." My God, may these words also be ours at our last hour—though they will not then have the same meaning and the same perfection. We are only worthless human beings; but granted our wretchedness, may they at least be ours as far as they can be.

What must I do if they are to be, O God? I must ask you what it is you have given me to do, and I must ask you—from whom alone strength comes—to do it. I beseech you, my Lord and my God, to let me see clearly what your will for me is. Then give me the strength to do it, fulfilling it loyally till the end, in thanksgiving and love.

—Blessed Charles de Foucauld, *The Spiritual Autobiography of Charles de Foucauld*

Love's
Victory

Matthew 28:1-10, 16-20

¹ After the sabbath, as the first day of the week was dawning, Mary Magdalene and the other Mary went to see the tomb. ²And suddenly there was a great earthquake; for an angel of the Lord, descending from heaven, came and rolled back the stone and sat on it. ³His appearance was like lightning, and his clothing white as snow. ⁴For fear of him the guards shook and became like dead men. ⁵But the angel said to the women, "Do not be afraid; I know that you are looking for Jesus who was crucified. ⁶He is not here; for he has been raised, as he said. Come, see the place where he lay. ⁷Then go quickly and tell his disciples, 'He has been raised from the dead, and indeed he is going ahead of you to Galilee; there you will see him.' This is my message for you." ⁸So they left the tomb quickly with fear and great joy, and ran to tell his disciples. ⁹Suddenly Jesus met them and said, "Greetings!" And they came to him, took hold of his feet, and worshiped him. ¹⁰Then Jesus said to them, "Do not be afraid; go and tell my brothers to go to Galilee; there they will see me." . . .

> To celebrate the Resurrection means that we believe in the love that does not fade even in death, that we know ourselves to be loved by the eternal love of God.
> —Anselm Grün,
> *Taste the Joy of Easter*

¹⁶Now the eleven disciples went to Galilee, to the mountain to which Jesus had directed them. ¹⁷When they saw him, they worshiped him; but some doubted. ¹⁸And Jesus came and said to them, "All authority in heaven and on earth has been given to me. ¹⁹Go therefore and make disciples of all nations, baptizing them in the name of the Father and of the Son and of the Holy Spirit, ²⁰and teaching them to obey everything that I have commanded you. And remember, I am with you always, to the end of the age."

(See also Mark 16:1-18; Luke 24:1-12, 50-53; John 20:1-18; Acts 1:3-11.)

Mark 16:19-20

[19] So then the Lord Jesus, after he had spoken to them, was taken up into heaven and sat down at the right hand of God. [20]And they went out and proclaimed the good news everywhere, while the Lord worked with them and confirmed the message by the signs that accompanied it.

T he astonishing event of the resurrection of Jesus is essentially an event of love," Pope Benedict XVI explained in his 2008 Easter address. It is "the Father's love in handing over his Son for the salvation of the world; the Son's love in abandoning himself to the Father's will for us all; the Spirit's love in raising Jesus from the dead in his transfigured body." Thus, the resurrection is the ultimate expression of the Trinity's intimate, personal love for us.

> **As partakers in the new life won for us by Christ, we too will one day be raised up and glorified with him.**

Mary Magdalene and her companion, "the other Mary," had come to the tomb to pay their last respects to Jesus' body. Both were among the faithful women who had followed Jesus from Galilee and stood steadfastly near the cross (see Matthew 27:55-56; Mark 15:40-41; Luke 23:49; John 19:25). As they approached the tomb, they were greeted by what is perhaps the most amazing announcement in human history: "He is not here; for he has been raised, as he said" (Matthew 28:6).

As he said. Indeed, Jesus had repeatedly told his followers that he was to suffer, die, and be raised up. Now everything that he had prophesized was coming to pass, just as it had been foretold in the Hebrew Scriptures that "the Messiah is to suffer and to rise from the dead on the third day" (Luke 24:46). In his first letter to the early church in Corinth, which was written before the gospels, St. Paul stressed the significance of the fulfillment of these ancient prophecies: "I handed on to you as of first importance what I in turn had received: that Christ died for our sins in accordance with the scriptures, . . . and that he was raised on the third day in accordance with the scriptures" (1 Corinthians 15:3-4).

None of the evangelists record that anyone witnessed the very moment and act of Jesus coming forth from the tomb. But when the angel rolled away the stone to show the women that the tomb was empty, there was a great earthquake (see Matthew 28:2). This upheaval reminds us that Christ's resurrection is an utterly earth-shaking and world-transforming event that affects the foundations of our lives. The resurrection rocked the earth, yet from this cataclysmic "event of love" came not destruction but hope, new life, and freedom from bondage to sin and death.

Jesus' female followers were the first to receive the announcement of the resurrection: "He is not here." Matthew, Mark, and Luke agree on this, and as Matthew recorded, after the angel had shown the two Marys the empty grave, he gave them a further message: "Go quickly and tell his disciples, 'He has been raised from the dead, and indeed he is going ahead of you to Galilee; there you will see him'" (Matthew 28:7). John's gospel gives Mary Magdalene pride of place as "the apostle to the apostles," sent by Jesus: "Go to my brothers and say to them, 'I am ascending to my Father and your Father, to my God and your God'" (John 20:17). The faithful women were the first to receive the good news and the first to pass it on to others.

As the bewildered Marys hastened from the tomb, "Jesus met them and said, 'Greetings!' And they came to him, took hold of his feet, and worshiped him" (Matthew 28:9). Overcome with joy, the two women knelt and clung to him. This was no vision, hallucination, or intangible spirit. Jesus' resurrected body was physical—real and tangible though indescribably transformed and glorified.

Jesus' ascension is his final glorification. Having fulfilled the Father's plan for our salvation, he returns to the Father, where he is exalted in glory. He has reached the end of his earthly journey of love, and has gone to prepare a place for us (see John 14:2). As partakers in the new life won for us by Christ, we too will one day be raised up and glorified with him.

But before he ascended to the Father, Jesus commissioned the apostles, "Make disciples of all nations, baptizing them in the name of the Father and of the Son and of the Holy Spirit, and teaching them to obey everything that I have commanded you" (Matthew 28:19-20). As Christ's followers today, we are called to take part in carrying out the threefold mission of evangelization, baptism, and teaching that Jesus entrusted to the Church more than two thousand years ago.

Understand!

1. Briefly summarize the two Marys' responses to Jesus' resurrection. How does Matthew describe their actions? Their emotions? What does his description suggest to you about the faith of the two women? About their relationship with Jesus prior to this encounter with him?

_____

_____

_____

_____

_____

_____

_____

2. What role and purpose does the angel play in Matthew's account of Easter morning? What does the angel's presence on the scene add to your understanding of this event? Why do you think God sent an angel to speak to the women before they actually encountered Jesus?

_____

_____

_____

_____

_____

_____

_____

3. Describe some of the properties of Jesus' physical body after he rose from the dead that are inferred in this passage. Read Luke 24:36-42 and John 20:19-20 for additional descriptions of the risen Lord. In what way(s) was Jesus' body changed after it had passed through death and was raised up?

_____

_____

_____

_____

_____

_____

4. What long-term effect(s) do you think Jesus' resurrection had on the lives of Mary Magdalene, "the other Mary," and those men and women to whom he later appeared? How is the commission given to the Marys by the angel (see Matthew 28:7) and by Jesus (see 28:10) related to the commission that Jesus gave to the disciples before he ascended (see 28:18-20)?

_____

_____

_____

_____

_____

_____

_____

5. Jesus promised his disciples, "I am with you always, to the end of the age" (Matthew 28:20). How has he kept this promise? In what way(s) is Jesus present in and to the Church today?

_____

_____

_____

_____

_____

_____

_____

▶ In the Spotlight
From the *Catechism of the Catholic Church*

"We bring you the good news that what God promised to the fathers, this day he has fulfilled to us their children by raising Jesus" [Acts 13:32-33]. The Resurrection of Jesus is the crowning truth of our faith in Christ, a faith believed and lived as the central truth by the first Christian community; handed on as fundamental by Tradition; established by the documents of the New Testament; and preached as an essential part of the Paschal mystery along with the cross:

> Christ is risen from the dead!
> Dying, he conquered death;
> To the dead, he has given life. (638)

"If Christ has not been raised, then our preaching is in vain and your faith is in vain" [1 Corinthians 15:14]. The Resurrection above all constitutes the confirmation of all Christ's works and teachings. All truths, even those most inaccessible to human reason, find their justification if Christ by his Resurrection has given the definitive proof of his divine authority, which he had promised. (651)

Faith in the Resurrection has as its object an event which as historically attested to by the disciples, who really encountered the Risen One. At the same time, this event is mysteriously transcendent insofar as it is the entry of Christ's humanity into the glory of God. (656)

Grow!

1. Why do you believe that Jesus was raised from the dead? How would you explain the basis of your personal faith in Jesus' resurrection to someone who is not Christian?

_____

_____

_____

_____

_____

_____

2. The women experienced fear and joy at the sight of the angel and the empty tomb. Do these two emotions seem compatible to you? Explain. In your opinion, are both fear and joy appropriate responses to the presence and/or action of God in your life? Why or why not?

_____

_____

_____

_____

_____

_____

3. What earth-shattering impact has Jesus' resurrection had on your faith? On your daily life? On your outlook toward the world around you? On your attitude toward the future?

_____

_____

_____

_____

_____

_____

4. In what way(s) have you seen the Lord "work with you and confirm the message" (see Mark 16:20) when you have shared the good news? With whom, in particular, would you like to share this news now? Ask the Holy Spirit to guide you in how to approach this person.

_____

_____

_____

_____

_____

5. How has your study of Jesus' passion and resurrection enhanced your personal relationship with him as your savior? As the Lord of your life? What might you do to continue to deepen your encounters with Jesus through Scripture and increase your understanding of God's word?

_____

_____

_____

_____

_____

The resurrection . . . is ultimately beyond our powers of explanation, for the resurrection is a sign of eternity. Christ's resurrection is not a scientific experiment but an act of divine power in which the laws governing our world are remade. No wonder the angel says of Jesus, "He is not here." God in Christ is already ahead of us. Just as Christ cannot be trapped in the tomb, so also he cannot be trapped by our limited understanding. Christ is already up and away, while like the women we struggle to grasp what has happened.

We can accept, but we cannot look for absolute proof, for who could squeeze eternity into time? Fortunately, we do not have to analyze in order to understand. There is another way: we can take up the story of the resurrection and make it part of the story of our lives.

—**Terry Tastard,** *Stations of the Resurrection:
The Way to Life*

Reflect!

1. The word "Lent" comes from the Anglo-Saxon *lencten,* which means "springtime" and shares the same root as the word "lengthen." Daylight grows longer during the season of Lent. Winter turns to spring, a time of rebirth and renewal in the world of nature. In the northern hemisphere, Christ's resurrection is celebrated in springtime, when new life blossoms forth. Indeed, the modern English term "Easter" comes from the Old English *Eastre,* originally referring to Eostre, the Anglo-Saxon goddess of the dawn and of the spring season. Her name was derived from the Indo-European root *aus,* which means "to shine" and has also given us the words "east" and "aurora."

Take a walk and feel the sun's light and warmth on you. Enjoy the world of nature, bursting with life. Rejoice and thank God as you see the power of the resurrection reflected all around you.

2. Read and reflect on the following Scripture passages to enhance your understanding of Jesus' resurrection and stir up your anticipation of the resurrection to come:

> Martha said to Jesus, "Lord, if you had been here, my brother [Lazarus] would not have died. But even now I know that God will give you whatever you ask of him." Jesus aid to her, "Your brother will rise again." Martha said to him, "I know that he will rise again in the resurrection on the last day." Jesus said to her, "I am the resurrection and the life. Those who believe in me, even though they die, will live, and everyone who lives and believes in me will never die."
>
> —John 11:21-26

> If Christ is proclaimed as raised from the dead, how can some of you say there is no resurrection of the dead? If there is no resurrection of the dead, then Christ has not been raised; and if Christ has not been raised, then our proclamation has been in vain and your faith has been in vain. We are even found to be misrepresenting God, because we testified of God that he raised Christ—whom he did not raise if it is true that the dead are not raised. For if the dead are not raised, then Christ has not been raised. If Christ has not been raised, your faith is futile and you are still in your sins. Then those also who have died in Christ have perished. If for this life only we have hoped in Christ, we are of all people most to be pitied.
>
> But in fact Christ has been raised from the dead, the first fruits of those who have died. For since death came

through a human being, the resurrection of the dead has also come through a human being; for as all die in Adam, so all will be made alive in Christ.

—1 Corinthians 15:12-22

The Lord himself, with a cry of command, with the arch-angel's call and with the sound of God's trumpet, will descend from heaven, and the dead in Christ will rise first. Then we who are alive, who are left, will be caught up in the clouds together with them to meet the Lord in the air; and so we will be with the Lord forever. Therefore encourage one another with these words.

—1 Thessalonians 4:16-18

When I [John] saw him, I fell at his feet as though dead. But he placed his right hand on me, saying, "Do not be afraid; I am the first and the last, and the living one. I was dead, and see, I am alive forever and ever; and I have the keys of Death and of Hades."

—Revelation 1:17-18

▶ In the Spotlight
In the Words of the Saints

Faith in the resurrection of Christ never misleads us, and hope in our own resurrection never deceives us, because God the Father both restored our Lord to life and will restore us to life too by virtue of his power.
—St. Bede the Venerable

Remember that the Passion of Christ ends always in the joy of the resurrection of Christ, so when you feel in your own heart the suffering of Christ, remember the resurrection has to come, the joy of Easter has to dawn. Never let anything so fill you with sorrow as to make you forget the joy of Christ risen.

—Blessed Teresa of Calcutta

Christ's Resurrection is our hope, and his Ascension is our glory. It was with his human nature that Christ entered heaven and sat on God's throne. This, therefore, is the raising and glorification of our human nature.

—St. Augustine

Act!

The women were charged by the angel, "Go quickly and tell his disciples, 'He has been raised from the dead'" (Matthew 28:7).

Ask yourself how well you are giving witness to Jesus' transforming power in your life through the ways you relate to family members, friends, co-workers, and neighbors. Do you openly share your faith with others? Do your words and actions build up and encourage others? Do you warmly show love and respect for others? Do you pray for and with them?

After you have examined yourself, ask the Holy Spirit to show you how you can creatively and actively express to others your faith and joy in the risen Lord. Resolve to share the good news with at least one person this week—then go do it!

▶ In the Spotlight
The Days between the Resurrection and the Ascension of Our Lord

Beloved, the days which passed between the Lord's resurrection and his ascension were by no means uneventful; during them great sacramental mysteries were confirmed, great truths revealed. . . .

Throughout the whole period between the resurrection and ascension, God's providence was at work to instill this one lesson into the hearts of the disciples, to set this one truth before their eyes, that our Lord Jesus Christ, who was truly born, truly suffered and truly died, should be recognized as truly risen from the dead. The blessed apostles together with all the others had been intimidated by the catastrophe of the cross, and their faith in the resurrection had been uncertain; but now they were so strengthened by the evident truth that when their Lord ascended into heaven, far from feeling any sadness, they were filled with great joy.

Indeed, that blessed company had a great and inexpressible cause for joy when it saw man's nature rising above the dignity of the whole heavenly creation, above the ranks of angels, above the exalted status of archangels. Nor would there be any limit to its upward course until humanity was admitted to a seat at the right hand of the eternal Father, to be enthroned at last in the glory of him to whose nature it was wedded in the person of the Son.

—St. Leo the Great

Practical Pointers for Bible Discussion Groups

A Bible discussion group is another key that can help us unlock God's word. Participating in a discussion or study group—whether through a parish, a prayer group, or a neighborhood—offers us the opportunity to grow not only in our love for God's word but also in our love for one another. We don't have to be trained Scripture scholars to benefit from discussing and studying the Bible together. Bible study groups provide environments in which we can worship and pray together and strengthen our relationships with other Christians. The following guidelines can help a group get started and run smoothly.

Getting Started

- Decide on a regular time and place to meet. Meeting on a regular basis allows the group to maintain continuity without losing momentum from the previous discussion.

- Set a time limit for each session. An hour and a half is a reasonable length of time in which to have a rewarding discussion on the material contained in each of the sessions in this guide. However, the group may find that a longer time is even more advantageous. If it is necessary to limit the meeting to an hour, select sections of the material that are of greatest interest to the group.

- Designate a moderator or facilitator to lead the discussions and keep the meetings on schedule. This person's role is to help preserve good group dynamics by keeping the discussion on track. He or she should help ensure that no one monopolizes the session and that each person—including the shyest or quietest individual—is offered an opportunity to speak. The group may want to ask members to take turns moderating the sessions.

- Provide enough copies of the study guide for each member of the group, and ask everyone to bring a Bible to the meetings. Each session's Scripture text and related passages for reflection are printed in full in the guides, but you will find that a Bible is helpful for looking up other passages and cross-references. The translation provided in this guide is the New Revised Standard Version (Catholic Edition). You may also want to refer to other translations—for example, the New American Bible or the New Jerusalem Bible—to gain additional insights into the text.

- Try to stay faithful to your commitment and attend as many sessions as possible. Not only does regular participation provide coherence and consistency to the group discussions, it also demonstrates that members value one another and are committed to sharing their lives with one another.

Session Dynamics

- Read the material for each session in advance and take time to consider the questions and your answers to them. The single most important key to any successful Bible study is having everyone prepared to participate.

- As a courtesy to all members of your group, try to begin and end each session on schedule. Being prompt respects the other commitments of the members and allows enough time for discussion. If the group still has more to discuss at the end of the allotted time, consider continuing the discussion at the next meeting.

- Open the sessions with prayer. A different person could have the responsibility of leading the opening prayer at each session. The prayer could be a spontaneous one, a traditional prayer such as the Our Father, or one that relates to the topic of that particular meeting. The members of the group might also want to begin some of the meetings with a song or hymn. Whatever you choose, ask the Holy Spirit to guide your discussion and study of the Scripture text presented in that session.

- Contribute actively to the discussion. Let the members of the group get to know you, but try to stick to the topic so that you won't divert the discussion from its purpose. And resist the temptation to monopolize the conversation, so that everyone will have an opportunity to learn from one another.

- Listen attentively to everyone in the group. Show respect for the other members and their contributions. Encourage, support, and affirm them as they share. Remember that many questions have more than one answer and that the experience of everyone in the group can be enriched by considering a variety of viewpoints.

- If you disagree with someone's observation or answer to a question, do so gently and respectfully, in a way that shows that you value the person who made the comment, and then explain your own point of view. For example, rather than saying, "You're wrong!" or "That's ridiculous!" try something like "I think I see what you're getting at, but I think that Jesus was saying something different in this passage." Be careful to avoid sounding aggressive or argumentative. Then watch to see how the subsequent discussion unfolds. Who knows? You may come away with a new and deeper perspective.

- Don't be afraid of pauses and reflective moments of silence during the session. People may need some time to think about a question before putting their thoughts into words.

- Maintain and respect confidentiality within the group. Safeguard the privacy and dignity of each member by not repeating what has been shared during the discussion session unless you have been given permission to do so. That way everyone will get the greatest benefit out of the group by feeling comfortable enough to share on a deep personal level.

- End the session with prayer. Thank God for what you have learned through the discussion, and ask him to help you integrate it into your life.

The Lord blesses all our efforts to come closer to him. As you spend time preparing for and meeting with your small group, be confident in the knowledge that Christ will fill you with wisdom, insight, grace, and the ability to see him at work in your daily life.

Sources and Acknowledgments

Session 1: Jesus' Entry into Jerusalem

Frank Sheed, *To Know Christ Jesus* (San Francisco: Ignatius Press, 1992), 318.

Fulton J. Sheen, *Life of Christ* (New York: Image Books/ Doubleday, 1990), 260.

Andrew of Crete, *Oration 9*, quoted in *The Liturgy of the Hours, Volume II* (New York: Catholic Book Publishing Co., 1976), 419.

Josemaría Escrivá, *Christ is passing by,* quoted in Francis Fernandez, *In Conversation with God –Volume Two* (London: Scepter Ltd., 1989), 248.

John Paul II, Palm Sunday Homily, 16 April 2000, http://www. vatican.va/holy_father/john_paul_ii/hom-ilies/2000/documents/hf_jp-ii_hom_20000416_palm-sunday_en.html.

Francis Martin, *The Fire in the Cloud: Lenten Meditations* (Ann Arbor, MI: Servant Publications, 2001), 122.

Session 2: The Last Supper

Ignatius of Antioch, http://www.acfp2000.com/Sections/ quotes1.html.

Irenaeus, quoted in Jill Haak Adels, *The Wisdom of the Saints: An Anthology* (New York: Oxford University Press, 1987), 81.

John Chrysostom, quoted in *The Wisdom of the Saints: An Anthology*, 82.

Cyril of Alexandria, *Homily 142*, quoted in R. Payne Smith, *A Commentary on the Gospel according to St. Luke by St. Cyril, Patriarch of Alexandria* (New York: Studion Publishers, Inc., 1983), 570.

John Gayton, "One Day in the Life of a Priest in Iraq," used with permission of CatholicMil.org, Catholics in the Military. All rights reserved. For more info, visit www.CatholicMil.org.

Josemaría Escrivá, *The Forge,* 828, http://www.opusdei.ie/art.php?p=12647.

Alphonsus Liguori, quoted in *Divine Love Came Down! Wisdom from Saint Alphonsus Liguori,* ed. Nancy Sabbag (Ijamsville, MD: The Word Among Us Press, 2003), 59.

Thomas Aquinas, quoted in *The Compact Catholic Prayer Book*, compiled by the editors of The Word Among Us Press (Ijamsville, MD: The Word Among Us Press, 2008), 53–54.

Père Jacques (Lucien-Louis Bunel), quoted in Francis Murphy, *Père Jacques: Resplendent in Victory* (Washington, DC: ICS Publications, 1998), 168.

John Paul II, Letter to Priests, Holy Thursday 2005, http://
www.vatican.va/holy_father/john_paul_ii/
letters/2005/documents/hf_jp-ii_let_20050313_
priests-holy-thursday_en.html.

Instruction on Eucharistic Worship: Sacred Congregation of Rites, 38, http://www.adoremus.org/
eucharisticummysterium.html.

SESSION 3: THE AGONY IN THE GARDEN

Basilea Schlink, *The Holy Places Today* (Darmstadt-
Eberstadt, West Germany: Evangelical Sisterhood of Mary,
1975), 6.

George Montague, *Mark: Good News for Hard Times* (Ann
Arbor, MI: Servant Books, 1981), 168.

Maria Boulding, *Prayer: Our Journey Home* (Ann Arbor, MI:
Servant Books, 1979), 4–5.

Raniero Cantalamessa, *Remember Jesus Christ: Responding
to the Challenges of Faith in Our Time*, trans. Marsha
Daigle-Williamson (Ijamsville, MD: The Word Among Us
Press, 2007), 96–97.

Josephus: Complete Works, The Wars of the Jews, Book 6,
Chapter 1.1, trans. William Whiston (Grand Rapids, MI:
Kregel Publications, 1982), 571.

Benedict XVI, General Audience, 4 April 2007, http://
www.vatican.va/holy_father/benedict_xvi/audiences/2007/
documents/hf_ben-xvi_aud_20070404_en.html.

Raniero Cantalamessa, 99.

Session 4: Jesus' Arrest and Trial

Ignatius Catholic Study Bible: The Gospel of John, with Introduction, Commentary, and Notes by Scott Hahn and Curtis Mitch; Study Questions by Dennis Walters (San Francisco: Ignatius Press, 2003), 51.

Henri Nouwen, "A Spirituality of Waiting," quoted in *Bread and Wine: Readings for Lent and Easter* (Maryknoll, NY: Orbis Books, 2007), 180–181.

Jeanne Kun, "The Judas in Me," *My Lord and My God! A Scriptural Journey with the Followers of Jesus* (Ijamsville, MD: The Word Among Us Press, 2004), 115.

Wendy Beckett, *Sister Wendy's Nativity* (Chicago: Loyola Press, 1998), 62.

Théophane Vénard, *A Modern Martyr,* revised and annotated by James A. Walsh (Ossining, NY: Catholic Foreign Mission Society, 1913), 180–181.

Stephen Binz, "The Crowds and the Authorities in the Passion Narratives," *God's Word Today,* (Volume 24, Number 3, March 2002), 46–47.

Session 5: Christ's Crucifixion

John Paul II, Address at Devotion to the Sacred Heart of Jesus, 7 June 1999, no. 2, http://www.catholic-forum.com/saints/pope0264xp.htm.

Wendy Beckett, *Sister Wendy's Nativity* (Chicago: Loyola Press, 1998), 78.

Benedict XVI, Letter on the Fiftieth Anniversary of the Encyclical *Haurietis Aquas* [On Devotion to the Sacred Heart], 15 May 2006, http://www.vatican.va/holy_father/benedict_xvi/letters/2006/documents/hf_ben-xvi_let_20060515_50-haurietis-aquas_en.html.

Ambrose, *Exposition of the Gospel of Luke 10.112–13,* quoted in *Ancient Christian Commentary on Scripture: Luke,* ed. Arthur A. Just, Jr. (Downers Grove, IL: InterVarsity Press, 2003), 363.

John Paul II, Homily delivered in Mexico, 26 January 1979, quoted in *The Navarre Bible: The Gospel of St. John,* with a commentary by the members of the Faculty of Theology of the University of Navarre (Blackrock, Ireland: Four Courts Press, 1995), 232.

Ambrose, http://campus.udayton.edu/mary/meditations/MotherofGod.html.

John of Ávila, quoted in *Virgin Wholly Marvelous: Praises of Our Lady by the Popes, Councils, Saints, and Doctors of the Church,* ed. David Supple (Cambridge, MA: The Ravengate Press, 1999), 76.

Josemaría Escrivá, *Christ is passing by*, 140, quoted in *The Navarre Bible: The Gospel of St. John*, with a commentary by the members of the Faculty of Theology of the University of Navarre (Blackrock, Ireland: Four Courts Press, 1995), 234.

Wendy Beckett, quoted in *In the Midst of Chaos, Peace*, compiled and edited by Daniel Thomas Paulos (San Francisco: Ignatius Press, 1999), 67.

Charles de Foucauld, *The Spiritual Autobiography of Charles de Foucauld*, ed. and annotated by Jean-François Six (Ijamsville, MD: The Word Among Us Press, 2003), 96.

SESSION 6: THE RESURRECTION

Anselm Grün, *Taste the Joy of Easter*, trans. Katherine Mistry-Tulloch and Andrew Tulloch (London: St. Paul's Publishing, 2002), 68.

Benedict XVI, Easter Message, 23 March 2008, http://www.vatican.va/holy_father/benedict_xvi/ mesages/urbi/documents/hf_ben-xvi_mes_20080323 _urbi-easter_en.html

Terry Tastard, *Stations of the Resurrection: The Way to Life* (Liguori, MO: Liguori Publications, 2007), 8–9.

Bede the Venerable, *Homily on the Gospels*, quoted in Rosemary Ellen Guiley, *The Quotable Saint* (New York: Checkmark Books, 2002), 230.

Mother Teresa, *Jesus, the Word to Be Spoken: Prayer and Meditations for Every Day of the Year,* compiled by Brother Angelo Devananda (Ann Arbor, MI: Servant Books, 1986), 36.

Augustine, quoted in Brother Victor-Antoine d'Ávila-Latourrette, *Blessings of the Daily: A Monastic Book of Days* (Liguori, MO: Liguori Publications, 2002), 208.

Leo the Great, *Sermo 1 de Ascensione,* quoted in *The Liturgy of the Hours,* Volume II (New York: Catholic Book Publishing Co., 1976), 898–899.

The Word Among Us
Keys to the Bible Series
For Individuals or Groups

These studies open up the meaning of the Scriptures while placing each passage within the context of the Bible and Church tradition.

Each of the six sessions features

- The Scripture text to be studied and insightful commentary
- Questions for reflection, discussion, and personal application
- "In the Spotlight" sections that offer wisdom from the saints, personal testimony, and fascinating historical background

Here are just a few of our popular titles:

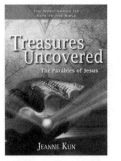 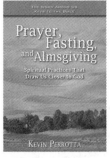 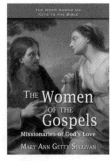 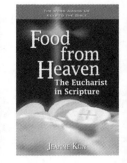

| Treasures Uncovered: The Parables of Jesus | Praying, Fasting, Almsgiving | Women of the Gospels | Food from Heaven: The Eucharist in Scripture |

Check out all the studies available in this series
by going online at **bookstore.wau.org**
or
call Customer Service at **1-800-775-9673**